Pure EQ: A Question Answered
By
Frank A. Bailey, M.Ed.

Chapter 1

"See? See what I mean?" My friend Jay gestured towards the ordering counter in the Mexican fast food chain restaurant. "That's the junk that I'm sick and tired of….why is it a guy like that can get a girl like that?"

I lowered my bean and cheese burrito momentarily and looked over in the direction that he was attentively despising. I noticed what he had. A somewhat plain guy in his late 20's with a stalky build, who was accompanied by a very slim and fit looking early 20's woman. It was clear that they had both come from working out, where he was sweaty and she had been perspiring. "What? Those two?" I asked.

"Uh, yeah." Jay snarked.

"Maybe they were just lifting together or he is her coach….. or they're good friends." I offered.

"Yeah, I don't think so. Look" Jay nodded in their direction.

The woman grabbed onto the stalky guy's sweaty, hairy arm and nuzzled in to whisper what I guessed was her order, followed by a giggle and a little peck on the cheek.

"Still think so?" Jay asked.

"Okay. Okay. So they're together. They apparently have something going, some things in common." I offered as I bit down into my burrito.

"All I'm saying is that if a guy like that can get a girl like that, then why can't I? I mean, I'm in shape! I take care of myself! I have a job, drive a sweet car, and I would treat her like gold!" Jay shook his head in frustration.

He was right on all counts. He was in pretty good shape, almost to a six pack ab status with a pretty good build overall. He had a mid-level salary position at a solid company, he drove a very sharp looking sports car, and he did treat every woman he dated like gold. So I chewed on it for a moment as I took another bite of my burrito. "I don't know." I said while I thought.

"Well, neither do I, but it's getting pretty freaking old. I bust my butt every day and try to stay in shape, then a guy like that walks in with her on his arm…dang! I just get tired of it!" Jay was getting fired up. When he got fired up he began to talk with one hand waving around wildly and the other on his hip – sitting or standing, one hand on his hip.

"I know you are. You just have to put yourself out there, you know. Watch for the signals and be open. Do some listening, ask the right questions. Just smile and be fun." I tried pitifully to offer the best advice that I had at the moment, but I was stuck on the question of why not.

"I've tried all of that and none of it works. You know what it is?" Jay asked.

"What?" I mumbled through another bite of my burrito.

"It's this area. There is no social scene in central Maine and I have to get out of here if I'm ever going to find anyone!" Jay was now waving very emphatically with his one free hand.

"So where are you going to go? You have a good job, a great car, and now you just need to do what you like to do and then you'll meet someone with that in common." I said matter of factly and almost convinced myself.

"Naw, I've tried that and it doesn't work. The women that are into ultimate Frisbee around here are too granola-ey (naturist) and the women that like mustangs either own one because they are in a midlife crisis or they're gold diggers. It's this area." Jay dismissed my halfhearted suggestions again.

"Well, maybe there are women throwing signals and you aren't seeing it." I countered.

"No way. I would know the moment she was into me." Jay glanced one more time at the couple picking up their tray and shook his head as he took his first bite. "I would see it." He said as he chewed.

I wasn't so sure. In fact, I would wager a bet that my friend had a particular type and the woman that was in the Mexican restaurant was what fit the bill! That's why he was so fired up about it.

The next week, Jay and I went to a bar and grill chain for a quick bite to eat. We were escorted to our table by our hostess, Jay had obviously noticed that she was an attractive young lady, as he was all smiles. She was polite, but professional. As she walked away, Jay said, "See? Now that's the kind of woman that I'm looking for!"

"No! She has to be at least 5 years younger than you!" I scoffed.

"Meh. Not a problem for me." He retorted.

Our waitress came to the table to welcome us and get us some drinks. She began the conversation with the usual offerings, but then I noticed something. She was tossing her hair back, she was making lingering eye contact with Jay, and she was doing a fair amount of smiling….she was into him! I began to get excited for my friend, as this was one of those times that I had been trying to get him to see. We both ordered and she said, "I'll get that right for you Hun. Be right back."

Jay didn't even notice! "Did you not see that she was throwing all of the right signals at you?!" I whispered as she walked away.

"Oh? I didn't notice anything. Besides, she's not really my type." Jay dismissed my comment.

"Oh come on! She was throwing all of the right signals at you! You had to of noticed! And right now, your type is standing with a pulse!" I exclaimed.

"I mean, she's cute and all, but she's a little bit bigger than I would prefer." Jay volleyed back.

"What? What? She can't be more than a size 12! Come on!" I couldn't believe what I was hearing.

"Yeah, I work hard to be where I'm at physically, so I want someone that will do the same. Besides, she's bigger than a size 12. I'm not being shallow, but there has to be something I'm attracted to if it's going to work." A sizzling shot back into my court.

"Okay, I can't argue the whole attraction thing, but you are coming off as really shallow. Why not just get her number and see where it leads? I'm not saying propose to her, for crying out loud, but at least do something!" I sent him a high lob.

Little did I know he would drop the racket and run off the verbal court on which we were skirmishing. "Yeah, I guess it's not her size. I don't know. It's just not clicking. I wish it would, but it's just not happening for me."

My jaw dropped. Our waitress came back and turned on the charm. She did everything to engage my friend, but because he had his mind made up, he completely missed an opportunity to have a relationship with a perfectly wonderful lady; friendship or otherwise.

We finished up our meal and she brought the check over to the table. "Will there be anything else?" she asked hoping.

"No, I'm good." Jay blurted.

Her disappointment was professionally veiled, but I could still detect a hint of hesitation as she lingered while she made small talk of thank you's and have a good evening. She walked towards the front of the restaurant and I urged Jay, "Come on."

"I told you. It's just not going to happen. I will leave a good tip, because she did do a great job. You good?" Jay asked.

"I guess so." I said as I gathered myself.

She met us at the door, held it open and wished him a good night. This woman was persistent, yet my friend just nodded, mumbled a thanks, and out the door he went. I nodded and gave a thank you rather emphatically. I could not believe what I had just witnessed.

I left that night wondering if he would ever find someone that he is attracted to and was attracted to him. I mean, what was he waiting for? What more could he want? Why wouldn't a woman that fit his ideal description be easier to find? There were many women that fit into this framework that he had mentally prepared, but they did not reach out the way this woman did. Why was she so emphatic in her persistence to make a connection with my friend, when he was not into her? Why does it have to be so difficult?

I now had a mission in mind. I was going to find an answer to Jay's question, why can't a guy like him get a girl like that? Why can't we be happy with what we have, why can't we know what someone else is thinking, and how do we get the relationships that we want out of life? Little did I know where these questions would take me.

My friend really does have a heart of gold and I do not fault him for having a guideline for what he considers attractive in a mate –you do too, if you are honest with yourself. In fact, we all measure our relationships of friends, partners, and acquaintances in very subtle ways, which are based off of how they make us feel. Sometimes we meet someone and we click, other times we just hear a person talk and as they grate on our last nerve, where we count the moments until we can escape. Why do some people elicit drastically different reactions out of us? Why can't we steer our reactions? What is it that makes us respond in the ways that we do?

I am an educator by trade, so I believe that anything can be taught, sometimes to my detriment. I started out as an educator working at a residential treatment facility for kids in crisis, where I learned very quickly to pay close attention to non-verbal cues and tone of voice. Non-verbal cues and tone of voice are those very subtle hints that we give off as we feel various emotions. Some people are better at masking these than others, but we all give hints to our true meaning of what we are saying through these non-verbal's and tone.

For example, someone can say "Hey" in a number of different ways. If I walk up to you and say "hey" in a light tone with high inflection, with raised eyebrows, a hint of a smile, and open arms – you would think that I am happy to see you. If I lean towards you with my eyebrows furrowed, the corners of my mouth turned down, and yelled "hey" loudly – you would know that I am angry. If I glanced over my shoulder at you, raised one eyebrow, nodded with a smirk, then said "hey" softly – you would know that I am flirting with you (not that I normally do that). So this is only one word, "hey", with three entirely different meanings based off of just non-verbal cues and the tone of my voice.

At the residential treatment facility I learned not only to read non-verbal cues out of a survival instinct, such as knowing when a kid is going to draw off and punch you without warning, but also to monitor my own non-verbal cues. These kids were pros at knowing which buttons to push and when to lightly tap them or drop a 10 ton wrecking ball on them! Once you get hooked, the word spreads fast and next thing you know, they all have your number and will push your buttons any time they please, for their amusement. You can't blame these kids, they are only doing what other damaged adults have already done to them, but much worse. So if you pursed your lips when you were frustrated, better watch out – they are onto you! If you tap your foot when you have nervous energy, they'll turn up the volume to watch you squirm! Get it under control, otherwise they will grind your buttons into powder and you will be burnt out before you know it! These were valuable lessons that I have never forgotten and would serve me well in the future!

So back to my friend's question and my quest. I began to track down information and devoured everything that I could get my hands on about interpersonal interactions. I began to look through all of the success literature. How to persuade people, how to make friends, how to this, and how to that. A lot of procedural guides that raise an awareness of how devoid I am of how and why my relationships are the way that they are, with no easy way to change it. There is nothing more frustrating than having an awareness of an issue and no solution. It's almost like having a fiberglass splinter.

Those of you who have ever installed fiberglass insulation without gloves, you know what I am talking about! For some reason, you can't feel that the fiberglass splinter is there while you are working with the fiberglass insulation, until after the fact, when you are washing up. As you are soaping up your hands, you will be sure to run your fingers over the invisible splinter, causing you to take pause and look for what you will not find. You shrug your shoulders and put your hands back in the sink and continue lathering up, when you nudge it again, but this time you know that something has to be there. You rinse your hands, hoping to find the source of the tenderness, only to see a red dot, where the fiberglass has caused irritation, but nothing to grab onto with tweezers. You run the hottest water that you can stand and hope that it will be enough to get it out, aware that this needs to be remedied immediately or the effect will be just enough to throw a monkey wrench into your daily routine. You think that the hot water did the trick, but eventually you will run your finger over it again and bring up that painfully sharp awareness of the issue time and again. Your awareness of the splinter increases, as the frequency of contact increases, but with no remedy in sight, it just takes time for the splinter to eventually break away and leave you knowing that the next time you insulate, you will have this joy to look forward to.

Awareness can be a very frustrating irritation, if a solution is not visible. This is what I found to be the case with all of the interpersonal skills books and articles that are too numerous to count. There are many wonderful resources, if you want an awareness of your inept ability to troubleshoot relationships. A treasure trove of relationship hacks that only work one dimension of an issue, leaving the other dimensions twisting in the wind. I discovered a list of resources that left me wanting in the worst way, frustrated beyond belief, and ready to quit my quest. So I would step away, but always return, like a dog to its vomit, slurping up more useless information.

I eventually moved to another company, but I would continue to plug away, especially when my boss would tell me that they want me to standardize operations for our company across two states, due to my "way with people". The standardization was a lengthy process that could have been trying for all involved, but due to my "professional and courteous acumen" I was able to navigate these treacherous waters of standardization implementation. I began to delve into my interpersonal relationship skills and abilities, when I developed a stark awareness that the only reason my boss told me that I have a way with people was to get me to do the work that no one else wanted to do, or so I thought. As disappointed as I was, I redoubled my efforts to see if there was some merit to what he had said. I found that this was the case, that I did have a way with people, but despite pulling on the lessons learned from the residential treatment facility about non-verbal cues and tone of voice, I still came up lacking.

So there I was at this new company, managing the facility, with three workers that could not seem to get along. One worker was extremely knowledgeable about the facility and processes with a great work ethic, but had horrible interpersonal skills due to a skewed sense of what was "fair". We will call him Mr. Fair. The second worker was diligent in his area, ensuring that an impeccable standard was kept, but needed a certain amount of autonomy to feel appreciated and continue in this manner – there was no issue in providing this, where he was a professional. We will call him Mr. Pro. The third worker had been in the facility for years and knew the business inside and out, but also knew the management inside and out, to the extent that he was very slick with his production numbers and interpersonal skills. We will call him Mr. Slick.

It seemed as though these three would never get along or play nice in the sandbox. Mr. Fair would take turns aiming his sites on the other two, stirring up things in the facility just enough to disrupt the flow of production. Then

Mr. Pro would become very angry and come to the office to complain that Mr. Fair was at it again and he was tired of his interference. Mr. Fair's contention was that Mr. Pro would not work in other areas, even when his work was done in his own area, but that he would sit in his cushy office and not help the other workers. Mr. Pro stated that he had a process and it involved a fair amount of paperwork to keep everything straight, so there were times where he was in his office, but it was productive. The situation would devolve into a back and forth bickering match – grown men mind you – until I had to separate them and tell them each to stay in their own areas.

Mr. Fair and Mr. Pro would oblige, remaining unwillingly civil to one another. Mr. Pro and Mr. Fair would go back to producing large quantities of quality product, but then it was only a matter of time that Mr. Fair would start to look in on Mr. Slick. Mr. Slick would get plenty of work done, making it look very easy, which infuriated Mr. Fair, who didn't always do things the most efficient way, but in a manner that pleased him, because he felt that he was working the hardest in the facility. Mr. Fair would then make comments about Mr. Slick in the break room and stir up trouble again. Mr. Slick wouldn't get riled up, yet he would redouble his efforts towards making Mr. Fair look very foolish. Mr. Fair would then run to complain about Mr. Slick's perceived lack of performance, to which I would state that his numbers were solid; this only infuriated Mr. Fair because he felt that I favored Mr. Slick and Mr. Pro over him.

I thought long and hard about how to manage these three high producing individuals. Each worker was extremely valuable, but they each had challenges that they presented daily. I did have an easier time getting along with Mr. Pro, because of his desired level of professionalism and dedication to impeccable record keeping, which made reporting our numbers to senior management a breeze. I got along with Mr. Slick because he would prioritize based off of what we needed at the time at a fairly low stress level, so long as I maintained and protected his autonomy to run his area; I could trust him to follow through. Mr. Fair would accuse me many times of favoritism, to which I would attempt to smooth over the relationship that I had with him and point out what I appreciated about him. Eventually Mr. Fair grew tired of my attempts to work this angle and one time accused me of working him over with smooth words. I was at a loss. What else was there to do to make these three get along, beyond just separating them?

The theme of interpersonal skill fluency was staring me in the face, yet again. How do I manage these three individuals? I sought out my senior management to get advice, expressing the need to get all three of these individuals to play nice in the sand box, or I would eventually have to replace Mr. Fair, where he was the most consistent stream of discomfort in the facility. Senior Management's advice was to roll with the demons you got, because when you bring in someone new, you have a whole new demon to work around.

This was the hallmark of the least helpful advice I have ever received about interpersonal skills and managing people.

The situation continued over the five years that I remained at that facility, where each and every day I could guarantee that someone would come to me with an interpersonal issue. It was a high stress environment, with dangerous work, and demanding customers. Before the day even started, tempers were already flaring due to outside pressures that faced each of my employees, but I was unable to help them find a better way to address these issues. My best was to separate them all under mountains of work, where my thought was if they have time to fight, then they don't have enough work. This was only a temporary solution to shift the focus of their frustrations to something productive, as I did the same thing.

Shifting your focus off of an awareness of an overwhelming issue onto something else does not solve anything, it only allows it to fester and become cancerous. The situation at the facility would sometimes erupt, coming just shy of physical altercations, but I would equip my best de-escalation techniques that I brought from the residential treatment facility work and band aid the pulsing wound. I know that you can't band aid arterial bleeding, but that was my role, day in and day out. I couldn't fire any of them, because I needed them and they didn't violate any company rules, so there we all remained, all of us miserable.

Don't get me wrong. There were some good times where we would laugh and have fun, but there was more conflict than there should have been, then what I should have allowed to continue. If I had of known then, what I know now, these three individuals would have had a much better work environment. If I had more than an awareness, I could have been a more effective leader, one that these three deserved. I failed them, because I was not equipped. I failed them because I did not have a way to teach them to be more in tune with our relationship choices, just a lot of curt advice, that never seemed to last. These three men have moved on for various reasons, but I wish that I could have had more of an impact and given them the gift of insight that I am giving to you through this book.

So let's take a break and do a quick exercise.

1. Take a moment and list ten people that you know. Be sure to include 5 that you really get along with (whom you choose to spend time with above all else) and five that you tolerate, but can't wait to get away from them. For example – you really like Johnny, but can't stand Suzy – list 5 of each.

2. Once you have your list, write down what you really like about all 10 of them in 5 words or less – I know that

it's tough for the tolerable ones, but still do it. For example – Johnny - respects what I say and Suzy - will listen anytime.

3. Next write down what really ticks you off about all 10 of them (5 word limit) – again, I know that it may not be easy for the 5 you like, but do it anyway. For example – Johnny - sometimes too busy to listen (which makes me feel bad) and Suzy - tells everyone everything/can't trust her.

4. Next, note what you think the motivation would be for the things that you really like about them. For example: Johnny respects me and that makes me feel like he appreciates me. Suzy will listen anytime, which also makes me feel like she has time for me.

5. Next, note what you think the motivation would be for the things that tick you off. For example – Johnny being too busy makes me feel bad because I'm not important as other things and Suzy is not trust worthy, which makes me feel like she doesn't value my friendship.

6. Now compare the lists – any common themes? See anything similar in what you like versus what you don't like? See anything that you do to others in either list? Why do these things make you happy or upset you?

7. It all comes down to two words: importance and value. Looking at the list of things that you really like,

when your friends do these things, do they make you feel important and valued? If they do the things that tick you off, do you feel unimportant and devalued?

Here is my first important and valuable finding: every relationship boils down to importance and value.

Chapter 2

"Oh my word! You are so stupid!"

"You don't even listen to me anymore!"

"Why do I even bother?!"

"You make me feel unimportant and devalued!"

Have you ever seen that game where one of these things don't fit in with the others? Yeah, this is it. Have you ever uttered one of the top three phrases or some rendition like them? Of course, we all have. Most likely you have done so, out of frustration stemming from another individual's actions, words, or choices. The reason that the fourth statement stands out is that no one really uses that terminology, but, at the core, it's what we all really mean. When we get upset, this is what we are really thinking, feeling, and sometimes saying. I'm not talking about minimally irritated, but truly upset, possibly even seeing red! When you are "seeing red" is when you physically lock up, your breathing speeds up and becomes shallow, and your field of vision closes in as your temperature rises. I have only seen red once and it is an experience that I do not want to repeat!

So how do we avoid "seeing red"?

It is all about importance and value. Businesses really use this to their advantage. If you think of your favorite fast food chain, how do they make you feel important and valued? They focus on these two things in very specific ways. They make you feel important by providing fast service, such as, getting your food to you as promptly and accurately as possible, thereby reinforcing that your time is important to them. They make you feel valued by providing low cost or high volume food, think dollar menu and supersize, reinforcing that you deserve the most and best that they can give you for your money. It works! If it didn't, would you go back? Of course not!

However, if you waited around for more than five minutes, received the wrong order, was charged too much, or received a smaller size, then you would most likely complain, because you now feel unimportant or devalued. Remember, in this fast food chain, your importance is all about time and accuracy, along with value being the cost and size. If either of those are off, we feel perfectly fine in strongly questioning the fast food chain's loyalty to customer service. Often times I have been waiting in line, when someone, who has felt unimportant and devalued, feels that they are now entitled to strongly voice their opinion…while still in line….loudly enough for the whole restaurant to hear….while yelling obscenities. Over the top? Absolutely! Out of line? You bet! Did that make him feel any less unimportant or devalued? Maybe when the management jumped to get him what he wanted, so that he would quiet down!

What we feel is, at the core, tied to our importance and value, which can change based on very simple factors. For example, if you were at an upscale dining establishment, you would not have an issue with waiting five minutes to be seated, in fact, there can be wait times of up to an hour, if you did not book a reservation. You do not get irate, because you expect this from the upscale dining establishment, so therefore it does not make you feel unimportant or devalued. You do not choose the table where you are going to be seated, you do not get frustrated by the wait time for the waiter, you do not get frustrated if dinner does not come out just so, you especially do not raise an eyebrow at the bill, because none of this is tied to our feelings of importance and value at this establishment. The ambiance and presentation of the establishment denotes importance. The cleanliness and professional wait staff denote value. Our expectations of importance and value have shifted, but why?

We can look at these two scenarios and just ignore the seemingly trivial details of what makes a good dining experience at each, but if we do, we miss a prime opportunity to peer inside our own thought process. Importance and value at the fast food chain was all about speed, accuracy, size of portions, and wait time. Importance and value at the upscale dining establishment was all about ambiance, presentation, cleanliness, and professional wait staff. Why are our expectations so different? Because we hold one in higher esteem than the other, we have different expectations. Why not wait in line for your dollar menu cheeseburger and fries for 30 minutes? You don't have time? But have you waited for thirty minutes in a sit down restaurant for a cheeseburger and fries? We all have, because that is what we expect! If we expect that it will take 30 minutes, then we plan for that to occur. If it takes longer, then we begin to get upset, less and we are elated, all based on our perceived expectations. Right or wrong, our expectations will play a large part of the degree to which we feel importance and value.

We place expectations on everything, everyone, and every moment of our day. When things do not go according to plan, what do we do? We get upset. When things go according, or better, than what we had planned, we are elated! The level of our dissatisfaction or satisfaction is determined by our level of expectation. If you drive up to a coffeehouse and see a long line that you did not expect, you are already upset, yet, if you walk into a chilled out, laid back coffeehouse serving up dark roast and playing soft indie music, then your lengthy wait time is mitigated by the expectation that it's supposed to take this long. So day in and day out we are choosing to set ourselves up to be disappointed by the level of our expectations.

So how do we set our expectations accordingly? This may sound confusing, but the answer is to be aware of your expectations before you get into a situation. If you know that a coffeehouse is slammed around 5:00AM, then either make coffee at home or go at 5:30AM after that first rush. If one of the baristas behind the counter is having a rough morning, take a moment and consider that your expectation of their professionalism is not their utmost concern, because they have 15 beverages that need to be made right now and more on the way. So if they don't call your name with sunshine beaming from their joyous face, don't rail on them, but beam sunshine from your joyous face and make their day a little brighter instead! They won't be expecting it, but it will make things a little less horrible for that one moment in time for them and make you a little happier for being grateful; not to mention that they may remember you and skip your drink up the line next time.

So when we approach any situation and we attempt to understand our expectations, we must take into account what we are thinking and feeling right then and there. This is extremely important and only comes with a lot of practice through reflection of breaking down what just happened. Have you ever blurted out something and wondered why in the world you just said that? Well, you don't have to spend a lot of intentional time reflecting, because it is highly likely that you will replay that scenario over and over again a hundred times, cementing it in your head. I remember one time, I observed a young man attempting to talk with a girl that he was infatuated with and when the group laughed, he let out a very loud, voice cracking pre-pubescent laugh that stopped everyone for a moment, while they turned and looked at him, then all started cracking up at the outburst. The poor guy was mortified, but couldn't stop until he caught himself, at which point he turned and abruptly left the group, feeling unimportant and devalued by his own actions. It was so heart wrenching, but you had better be sure that he wondered why he did that over and over again, replaying the scenario, so as not to repeat it ever again.

When situations are incredibly awkward or uncomfortable, making us feel unimportant or devalued we tend to replay them, over and over, so as to ensure that this does not happen again. The difficulty is that we often focus only on our lessened social status and who to blame for the episode. Our tactic is only part of the way there. What really needs to happen is to start with personal responsibility when reflecting on what were we thinking and feeling and how did we display that to others. If the poor guy that had the laughing fit took a moment to determine the level of laughter within the group, instead of his preoccupied fixation on the girl of his affections, then he would have picked up that his volume should be that of a chuckle. I have found that taking a brief moment to think about what you are going to do, or are currently doing, can go a long way towards getting your feelings in the right place as well.

Our thoughts are the breeding grounds for our success or failures. Whatever we think will determine how we feel. What we feel will determine how we act. How we act will become what we are known for in our conduct. Our conduct will become our reputation. How do we want to be known? Do we want to be that irrational individual that laughs too loud and then awkwardly runs off due to embarrassment? Do we want to be that individual that chuckles just loud enough to be noticed, so that we can start a conversation with the individual of our interest? This is all a matter of our choosing to stop and think about the world around us with intention to purposely choose what we desire to occur. This doesn't mean that just because we are being intentional in our actions, that our every dream will come true, but it's more so an attempt to spend some time beforehand to minimize our undesirable actions within that situation.

I'm not talking about visualization. I'm talking about intentionally choosing how you will respond in a situation. A lot of people have told me that they can't think that fast in the moment. Of course not. When you are faced with the situation to make a decision on the spot, it is already too late to begin thinking about what am I going to do here? This is why the 100 meter sprint Olympic track stars practice their block starts over and over again. This is the point of the race that will either make or break you – a bad start is the end of your race! They take their time and focus deliberate intention when practicing their block starts over and over again, until it becomes muscle memory – a well-trained response. They are aware of where every limb is positioned, when every muscle contracts, and where their body is in time and space, that way when they get to the Olympics, it is just a matter of stepping into the blocks and waiting for the gun to go off. It is also up to you to practice the skill of reflecting on what you are thinking and what you are feeling, so you too can have a well-trained response.

So let's take another look at the expectations and interactions between the three workers at the facility I was managing. Mr. Fair was thinking that everything needs to be fair and that carried over into what he felt, which was passion for fairness and when he saw someone else that he perceived was less busy than he was, he became upset. Mr. Fair did not have an unreasonable expectation, that everyone should do their fair share, but the way that he was thinking about the situation determined his feelings and actions. Mr. Fair thought that Mr. Pro was just sitting and relaxing in his cushy office chair, doing "paperwork", which led him to think that Mr. Pro was lazy and not doing his fair share. When Mr. Fair called out Mr. Pro on not doing his part, Mr. Pro's response was shock, surprise, and insult. Mr. Pro prided himself on his professionalism and quality, which took time, so he became very defensive when accused of being lazy and not doing his fair share – he worked very hard! Mr. Pro thought that Mr. Fair was nosy and didn't have any idea about what it took to do this job, so when Mr. Fair proposed that Mr. Pro help out elsewhere, that "help" would cut into Mr. Pro's ability to do a quality job, an expectation that he had placed upon himself. Both Mr. Fair and Mr. Pro started off with thinking that did not take into account personal responsibility, they did not consider what message they were sending to others day in and day out, which led to a strained work environment.

Mr. Fair and Mr. Slick were sadly on the same track of looking at the other and not accounting for their own personal responsibility in the situation. Mr. Fair thought Mr. Slick was not working hard enough, which made Mr. Fair feel like Mr. Slick was producing less than the amount of work that he felt was adequate, based on his own expectations. Mr. Slick did not see the need to work in a wasteful manner, like Mr. Fair, but instead thought how foolish it was to do all of the extra work that Mr. Fair did every day while completing his process, based on his own expectations. These thoughts resulted in Mr. Fair feeling that Mr. Slick was not producing enough and trying to get away with not working hard enough and Mr. Slick feeling that Mr. Fair was a fool for doing so much extra work all of the time. Neither one wanted to listen to the other, which is unfortunate, because they could have really helped each other out in very tangible ways. Due to their ideal expectations and incorrect thinking, they continued to feed the cycle of unimportance and devaluing one another.

Mr. Fair, Mr. Pro, and Mr. Slick all thought and felt things that were not accurate, due to simply starting with what they expected the other guy "should be" doing. If they had of stopped and thought about personal responsibility – what they should be doing – then they would have started off with right thinking, which would have turned into right feeling, then right actions. If Mr. Fair had of been more concerned with his quality of product, he would have asked Mr. Pro for his perspective and help. At that point, Mr. Pro might have realized that he could help in ways that would not negatively impact his quality production, at the same time Mr. Pro might have become aware of the message that is sent when he stays in his office completing paperwork. If Mr. Slick would have taken a little bit of his time that he had conserved and used it to help Mr. Fair become more efficient, then Mr. Fair would have not second guessed what Mr. Slick was doing with all of his extra time, because he would have had extra time as well. The issue is that they all had preconceived expectations of what the other should have been doing, instead of taking a moment to consider their role and personal responsibility.

Again, when we start with personal responsibility, aka, what am I thinking and feeling and what message does it send to others, it starts us off with right thinking. Right thinking will turn into right feeling. Right feeling will lead to right actions. Right actions will turn into right conduct. Right conduct will become right reputation. Mr. Fair had a reputation for being a troublemaker, looking at everyone else, instead of minding his own business. Mr. Pro had a reputation for staying in his cushy office chair, instead of helping others. Mr. Slick had a reputation of not producing enough, when he could have helped others be more productive and efficient. Just imagine how things could have changed if they put personal responsibility first, determined how they could have made the others feel important and valued, even after the altercations, and then acted upon that information. Everyone's expectations may have changed and the facility would have become way more productive and enjoyable!

When you have a situation that you are either feeling unimportant or devalued because of somebody else's words or actions, take a moment and consider if there was some component that resulted because you had neglected your personal responsibility. Were you part of the issue that upset that person? What did you do or say? Also what did you not do or what did you not say? Omission can also make someone feel unimportant or devalued if they were expecting acknowledgement. Can you honestly say that you had no part in this individual's feeling like they have been devalued? Whether you meant it or not, it does not matter, but how can you live peaceably, as much depends upon you? I am not saying that you should be foolish with this and get walked all over, but what can you do to mitigate the consequences of the interaction that was just had and come out with a peaceable solution on the other side?

A word of caution. There are some individuals that are looking to take advantage of you or will not reciprocate the kindness that you attempt to show them. There is an old saying, "Don't cast your pearls before swine, lest they turn and trample them." If you are attempting right thinking/feeling/actions and the other party is just being nasty and trampling on your "pearls", then do not retaliate, but simply remove yourself from the situation as soon as you can reasonably do so. Living peaceably is not easy, I never said it was nor will I stake that claim, but it will lead towards a much better reputation, with far better consequences in the long run. In my daily activities, as I seek to make each person I interact with feel important and valued (yes, every single person, even the difficult ones) I find that this is not an easy task and I do not always succeed. This is where reflection on what I was thinking and feeling and what did I do comes into play; what was my personal responsibility? I look at it like this: was I right or did I get results?

In a difficult and/or contentious interpersonal situation, I always remember to ask myself, am I right or am I going to get results. The issue here is that being right feels great and getting results doesn't always feel good, at first. Until you realize what kind of damage you have caused and once you have to go back and repair that relationship that you have unknowingly imploded. Rebuilding a burnt bridge is not fun, because you and the other side are more than likely to have been burnt in the process. Even a superficial burn is extremely painful during the healing process. A first degree sunburn is painful and uncomfortable and during the time that it is healing, you are very sensitive to touch. The slightest amount of pressure, even when meant to be an encouraging hug, can elicit quite the reaction! Depending on the extent of the damage caused by the implosion of the relationship, you may be carefully rebuilding for a very long time!

As you walk into a situation where you know that you can either be right or get results, take a moment to reflect on how you want the conversation to play out.

What do you anticipate the other party will have for contentious issues?

How do you plan to respond to them?

What happens when things do not go your way?

What is your ultimate goal?

Where do you really want to get and how do you plan on getting there?

Intentionally think about these things before the meeting, that way, you already have the personal responsibility of how am I going to work though this to achieve the results that I desire? How am I going to demonstrate importance and value of the other party's ideas, thoughts, and feelings? This will determine how you think about the other party, possibly with an allied mindset, instead of adversarial. It will then play out in your actions, to the extent of allowing you to roll with the punches, even if you didn't consider what was to come, you were still mentally prepared to deal with conflict and get results! You still knew where you wanted to end up, as opposed to how you would fight to be right! You will get so much closer to your destination and your goal of getting results!

If you are in the moment and did not have time to prepare for the interaction, be mindful of your thoughts, feelings, and actions, trying to reflect as you go. This is not the easiest thing to do, but as you practice your reflective skills, it becomes easier and more innate. I was at the production facility and was scheduled to walk the facility footprint after a very large project, which I knew that I had gone over budget on, but had been within the allowed percentage for overage. I was confident in my work of coordinating the project when I stepped out to meet with the senior manager. We walked the project area and when we came to the spot that he had expected to be completed, he was visibly annoyed by the lack of progress. He questioned why it was not completed and commented quickly that we were already over budget and the one section that he wanted completed was not done! In the moment I could have said a number of things to correct his statements, so I would have been right, but I also would have risked my employment at this facility if I had ignored my personal responsibility in neglecting his expectations. I apologized and asked how he would like to proceed, in essence, seeking out how I could make it right. This surprised him and took him off guard, as he lit up a cigarette and began to reflect. His non-verbal cues and tone softened as he began to ask questions, eventually finding that, even though there was an overage in the budget, it was not as bad as he thought. The work that my senior manager had wanted done first was going to be completed within the following week; he also recognized that this full time project was given to me on top of my already demanding role. I had managed to get results in the moment due to right thinking, which led to right feeling, which played out in right actions. My senior manager then trusted me more, because he knew that I would be honest, I would step up, and I would take responsibility to do the right thing, even though it was not always the easy way – I was in it to get the right results.

Speaking of right results, let's take another look at Jay and his thought process. His goal was to be in a relationship with a woman that fit his ideal criteria. This is central to the issue at hand, a woman that fit his criteria. He wasn't focused on meeting a woman that he had something in common with, someone that he could enjoy spending his days with, not at all. He wasn't focused on finding a relationship that he could give as much, if not more than, the other person was willing to give. Jay was focused on finding someone that could fulfill only what he wanted. Jay was not focused on personal responsibility, which would have started with looking at another individual and seeing what you can offer up to make their life better, how you could make someone feel important and valued. He did not start with right thinking, so he did not have right feelings, which means that he did not have right actions, which is why he did not find "the" relationship. If we are only setting out to have all of our relationships and interactions fulfill our ideals, then we are setting expectations that no one can fulfill. However, if we are looking to start with that personal responsibility of making others feel important and valued, then we will have right thinking/feeling/actions that will have an impact of getting results that are very desirable.

It's time for an exercise. I will warn you - if you choose not to do this exercise, you will not get as much out of this chapter as you could!

1. Take your previous list of 10 individuals from Chapter 1's exercise. Look at the list again and review what you had written. Got it? Good.

2. Now, think of a previous interaction that was contentious for 3 of the 5 people that you get along with and 3 of the 5 that you tolerate, so that you now have a total of 6 "contentious" interactions overall. Put yourself in the role of an observer and write down a short description of each of these interactions, just the specific observable facts. What did you see, what did you hear, etc.

3. Once you have the facts written down, take a moment to reflect on what you were thinking and write it down for each – only your thoughts.

4. Now write down one word to describe how you were feeling.

5. Now write down what color that represents. If you were happy the color could be green, sad the color could be blue, etc.

6. What was the texture of the color? Was it spiky, sharp, smooth, like sand?

7. Now trace out the path of personal responsibility: what were you thinking? How did that impact what you were feeling? What did you end up doing as a result? What was the effect on your relationship?

8. Did this interaction make you feel important and valued? Did it make the other person feel important and valued? Why or why not? If one of you were devalued, what could you have done differently (only you, not the other person – personal responsibility)?

9. Do you see any themes to things that upset you? Try to describe them in one word.

Again, when we think of importance and value, we must remember what we can do in that interaction that rests upon us to live as peaceably as we can, taking personal responsibility to demonstrate importance and value to the other person, thereby exhibiting right thinking/feeling/actions and getting the results we want. Looking at the list of interactions that you have recorded, are there consistent things that tick you off, where you feel unimportant and devalued? If so, these may be your internal values that, when trampled, set you off the deep end faster than anything else, which is my next important finding.

Chapter 3

"I need you to take out the trash please! This is the third time I have asked you!" Jim's wife Kay didn't sound impressed to find the garbage bag still sitting where she had left it.

"I will. I just have to do one more thing." Jim retorted.

"No one more thing honey! This needs to go out, right now!" Kay demanded.

I could see that Jim's blood was starting to boil as he was setting down the skill saw. He had one more cut to finish up the project that he had been working on for his anniversary and then he could put down the saw and do the dump run. He took a deep breath, shook it off, and said, "I love my wife. I love my wife. I…love…my…wife."

Jim shot me a glance, as if to say get ready, because sparks may fly. Jim walked up to the front steps and opened the door to the kitchen and I could hear Kay question what he was doing. "Why would you be puttering out in the garage all this time, when you know that we have so much to do in here? We have the dump run that needs to be done, the trim boards to put up, curtain rods that need to be raised, I need to clean my office, and the kids all need lunch, so which do you want to do?" She questioned.

Jim bit his lip and just grabbed the garbage bag and turned to the door without saying anything, because what he wanted to say would not have gotten the results that he wanted, which was to quietly finish his project to surprise Kay. He closed the door a bit harder than he meant to and he paused for a moment, but then kept walking towards the garbage bins to load them into his pickup truck. Just as he got to the garbage bins, the door sprung open and out came Kay, just as irate as he was! She looked at him, dead in the eyes, and said "Now that was uncalled for…. You didn't even give me a kiss!"

Jim leaned over to give her a peck on the cheek, but she was not taking no for an answer. She grabbed onto Jim and planted one on him that made me look the other way, so much so that once she was pleased with herself, Jim had a big, goofy grin on his face. "I'll see you when you get back from the dump. Can you stop and grab some pizza sauce at the store please?" she cooed.

"Sure thing, my dear." Jim was turned right around where he stood.

Jim looked at me, shrugged, and said, "What are you gonna do?"

The relationship between Jim and Kay is very strong and even though there may be times that they are both extremely busy, they still make sure that they demonstrate importance and value towards one another. Jim and Kay get frustrated with each other, because they have busy lives and things don't always go the way that they want. Ultimately, they both know that they want the best for each other and they strive to make that happen constantly. This is not something that occurs naturally or passively. This is an intentional effort to ensure that they don't lose the other to misgivings of incorrect thinking/feeling/actions. So with all the right intentions, why on earth do they still get frustrated with each other?

As human beings, we are designed to have a response to stimuli, such as pain and pleasure. If something hurts, we don't want to do that anymore, just as a hand on a hot stove top is removed quickly. If something feels good, we want to do it all the more, like when someone scratches that hard to reach spot in the middle of your back, you don't want them to stop until that itch has been thoroughly scratched! We also have responses to stimuli that are automatic, which are key to our survival and originate in the amygdala. I'm not going to get too in depth, so just remember that there is a thinking part of your brain and an automatic response part of your brain that deals with filing away and recalling emotions, which is called the amygdala. This amygdala is responsible for the fight, flight, or freeze response when we sense danger.

This is best portrayed in viral videos of people being surprised, usually during Halloween. The scene is set, the unsuspecting victim is wandering precariously close to the trap, and then whamo! The trap is sprung! The responses vary greatly, from kids freezing in their tracks, to men sprinting in the opposite direction, and even grandmothers that come out swinging! No matter the situation, when we are surprised, it will elicit one of these responses. The same thing can happen on a much more subtle scale, depending on the stress level of the situation. In a situation where there is an extreme scare, such as the aforementioned prank, the stress level is very high, so the response is magnified. However, if the stress level is low, it may not lead to a full blown fight, flight, or freeze, but the level of stress will begin to accumulate. As more stress is added, the likelihood that the flight, flight, or freeze response will take over.

Here is an example. You wake up feeling very rested, when you roll over and see that you had shut off your alarm during the weekend and you are now running 45 minutes behind. Your stress level has just increased. You jump out of bed and rush to the bathroom, stubbing your toe on the doorframe…more stress. You finally get into the bathroom and decide to brush your teeth while showering to save time, which pans out, so you start to feel a little bit better and the stress level decreases. You then rush to get dressed and get your clothes out, but quickly discover that the shirt you had planned on wearing is seriously wrinkled, so now you have to pick out a completely different outfit…stress increases. You go out to get your morning coffee and see that at least the timer on the coffee maker was set right…stress lowered. You take your first sip of coffee and due to the fact that it has been on for a while, the coffee is the temperature of the sun and you burn your lips and tongue…stress increased. You rush out to your car and realize that today is the day of the big meeting and you won't have the time to prepare that you had thought you would…stress increased. You are speeding off to work and someone cuts you off and drives 5 miles per hour under the speed limit…stress substantially increased. Things continue like this throughout the day, where it increases and decreases, until you get home and are ready to tear someone's head off if they look at you wrong. This is stress accumulation that prepares you for the fight, flight, or freeze response if just one more thing happens to push you over the edge.

That's when it does. That one more thing to push you over the edge. It could be the dog chewing on your slipper, it could be the kids yelling as they run through the house, it could be spilling a glass of water that pushes you over the edge and then you snap. Once this occurs, it produces an undesirable reaction, where you are not thinking right, you are not feeling right, and you definitely do not act right! Ensuring that others feel important and valued is not at the top of your list, nor is it going to be, unless you do something about it. So what do you do? First off, you have to recognize that your physical movement is locking up, your breathing rate is getting faster and shallower, and you're beginning to see red; you are now primed to be emotionally hijacked. The emotional hijack is where that fight, flight, or freeze response takes over and you do a lot of damage in relationships. If you can cue into what is happening, take a deep breath, move around a bit, and say something out loud to get your mind off of it. Much like Jim did in the beginning of this chapter.

Jim had an accumulation of things that led him towards being frustrated with Kay's requests, which were not unreasonable, but it interfered with what he was trying to do at the moment. Kay had no idea what he was doing, she just knew that he was puttering out in the garage and she states exactly that. How would she know? He's trying to work on a surprise for her and he just can't seem to get it done. Both Jim and Kay have the best intentions, but the demands on their time are ramping up and they need each other to make it through. Both Jim and Kay reach a critical moment where either one of them could be hijacked, but Jim recognizes this in his self and keeps his peace (living peaceably), but Kay also recognizes what is going on and seeks to diffuse the situation by demonstrating very clearly that Jim is important to her and their relationship is valuable by planting a kiss on him right then and there! What a wonderful way to deescalate a situation…if only it were always that easy.

Often times there are a multitude of factors that play into why we get hijacked, but it can be traced back to the things that we hold dear, the things that we believe to be at the core of our very being, the things that we pride ourselves on doing each and every day. These core facets comprise the values that we hold most dear and if they are violated, then that can result in a hijack as well. Jim was getting close to being hijacked because Kay was questioning what he was doing with his time, implying that Jim was being wasteful with his time; Jim values integrity and being productive. Kay was getting close to a hijack because she needed support from Jim in the form of help with the list of household duties and when Jim slammed the door, she was hurt by his abruptness; Kay values support and caring within a relationship. Either one could be hijacked by what they were thinking and feeling or what they believed the other was thinking and feeling.

In the previous chapter we talked about personal responsibility, where we focused on what the individual can do to ensure that they demonstrate importance and value through right thinking/feeling/action aka what were they thinking and feeling and how can they show that. Now comes the next piece where you begin to take into consideration what the other person is thinking and feeling, as evidenced by their actions or how they are showing it. We cannot know anyone else's motivation for doing what they do, even if they tell us, we cannot truly know that what they have described is the ultimate truth in the situation, so we have to go strictly by specific observable behaviors.

Specific observable behaviors are tangible. This is what you can see and hear without adding motivation. I liken it to describing how a good or bad smart phone operates. If I told you that my smart phone is horrible since the last update, you would want to know why, because without something specific and observable, you only have my opinion. If I then follow that statement of indictment with "my smart phone is horrible since the last update, because it won't hold a charge and crashes every time I open up a web browser." You could agree then that this is an obvious sign of a pretty horrible phone, now that I have told you specifically what I have observed. The same goes for positive observations, where if I told you that my smart phone is amazing, then left you hanging, you would want to know what is so amazing about it, right? If I told you my amazing smart phone held a charge for 48 hours, you would probably want to run out and buy the same phone! So when you think of specific observable behavior, think of what you can see and hear, not so much the motivation behind it – you don't need the why, because it is distracting from the reality of what just happened and too hard to identify accurately.

This also saves you the trouble of determining the motivation behind someone's actions, which always involves judgement and that gets messy quick. If Kay had judged Jim's motivations, there was no way that she would have been correct, because she did not know that Jim was working on an anniversary gift and only would have made the situation worse. We can do the same when we begin to judge motivation, where it will only make the situation worse than if we just stuck to what they said and did; they can't argue with that! So when looking for cues as to what the other person is thinking and feeling, ask them if you can't figure it out. You can say, "That's interesting, why do you say that?" This gives you time to calm down a little bit and listen to the other person to figure out what is going on beyond the words and actions, possibly more insight into how to demonstrate importance and value to the other side.

So another crucial component to consider is that when someone is coming at you and you are getting close to that hijack, just consider for a moment that they, their self, are hijacked! This can become quite the predicament, where both parties are hijacked and no one is pausing to think about their personal responsibility. So if you can cue into the signs of physical lock up, increased breathing that becomes shallow, and that seeing red gaze in the other person, this is sure to signal that you need to do something to side step the impending doom and cue into what makes them feel important and valued. This is exactly what happened with Jim when he was standing out at the garbage bins, all locked up and breathing quick and shallow, that is until Kay came up to him and reminded him that he is important and valuable to her. It might not be Kay's first action of choice, but she knew how to get results and melt the one that she loves. What can we do to deescalate the situation and keep the potential for an emotional hijack as low as possible?

Hopefully you are now thinking of a previous situation in one of the interactions from your Chapter 2 list. You have recorded quite a bit of information about the interaction already, where you have what you were thinking and feeling, what made you feel unimportant and devalued, what made the other person feel unimportant and devalued, what was the result, and what would you have done differently. Also we looked at themes of things that upset you and you tried to describe them in a few words. These would be the descriptors of your core values. Remember with Jim that he values integrity and being productive, while Kay values support and caring within a relationship. The reason that it is important to define these core values is to increase your awareness of the reasoning behind why you personally experience an emotional hijack.

What is it that sends you to the moon in less than a second?

Maybe it's a couple of things? Take a moment and really think about it and don't skirt the issue. Boil it down and marinate on it, then try to describe it in one word. Is your core value integrity, hard work, or autonomy? Have you ever had a supervisor make you very angry over a line of questioning that you took very personal for some odd reason? Have you ever been in a relationship where your partner questions where you were, suggesting that something is not quite as it seems? Have you ever been questioned by a parent for being out where they think you should not have been, but you were emphatic that you followed the rules, however, you still got very upset? These are all emotional hijacks that stem from our core values being called into question, which makes us feel unimportant and devalued. We feel unimportant, because we begin to think that the other person has no idea what they are talking about and they have no right to treat us that way! You both had expectations of the other and it's starting to look like both sides could be very easily disappointed! When this happens, we feel devalued because what we hold dear is now called into question by their underlying accusations! We are prime for an emotional hijack!

The other side to this is that the individual that is questioning you is also primed for an emotional hijack, depending on your response. I'm not just talking about the words that you will respond with, but the tone that you inflect as you utter that rebuttal, the non-verbal cues that are either confirming or condemning in the eyes of your accuser. This can be a set up for a very negative interaction, unless you clue into the non-verbal cues and tone within the interaction. Again, what are you thinking and feeling, how are you displaying that, what is the other person thinking and feeling, how are they displaying that, how is each party feeling unimportant or devalued, and what can you take personal responsibility for to demonstrate that the other party is important and valued? It doesn't feel good, because you could easily be right, but what do you want the result to be here? You can be right and end up damaging that relationship.

This leads me to a very important component to building healthy relationships. If you are lying, stop it! This is like cancer to a relationship. It starts out small, then grows out of control and eventually the relationship is on life support, dying a slow and painful death, where all parties are left to grieve. Even if the cancer is cured, the relationship will never be the same. There will always be the fear that the cancer (lying) will come back, so do yourself a favor and don't lie. If you feel that you have to lie in a relationship, then you should sincerely ask yourself why you are in that relationship for starters? Is it a self-seeking purpose, where you are getting something for nothing? Did it start out great, but then you found that the other party misrepresented from the beginning by lying to you? What is the reasoning for the lying? If lying is a tactic that you have chosen to employ, then you have begun to base decisions on emotion and not on personal responsibility through right thinking – there will be no good that can come from this.

Right thinking will grow into right feeling, right feeling will grow into right actions, right actions grow into right conduct, and right conduct grows into right reputation. If you start out with the intention to lie, then you will be known as a liar – is this your goal? I should hope not, because even politicians strive to not be seen as a liar and this is almost always an expectation of the profession! If this is your goal, then you already know that you will eventually be found out, because you do not value the relationship nor do you feel that the other person is important;, there will always be trouble where ever a lie takes root. This is the fastest way to ensure that the other individual will feel unimportant and devalued, because you are giving something false to another person, who expected it to be genuine and true. The issue here is that their expectation was not unreasonable, yet you have provided them with a falsehood and sought to undermine their reasonable expectation from the beginning.

If you go on a rollercoaster, what is your expectation? That it will be a thrilling and high speed ride, maybe with a couple of loops and plenty of sharp turns and hills; most importantly you expect it to be safe and free from defects. You expect that a safety check was performed that morning, just like it should have been performed each and every morning. You expect that routine maintenance has been performed on schedule and that everything is top notch before you even walk through the amusement park gate. You expect that the warnings posted are there to promote top notch safety and that you will have an amazing ride that is fun and safe. If you did not expect all of this, would you get on the rollercoaster ride? If you knew it was unsafe, if it was not checked every morning, if it was not maintained, and had a reputation for causing injury, would you even risk stepping into line? Of course not! The end result of an unsafe rollercoaster is the eventual shut down of that ride, so that the safety specifications can be met, proper maintenance can be performed, and people's expectation of a thrilling and safe ride can be met.

So don't be a defective rollercoaster! You may appear to be thrilling and fun, but you had better be what you advertise yourself to be, otherwise you will eventually end up with a mess on your hands! Then you will continue the cover up, until it reaches such a magnitude that you cannot possibly continue and the relationship reaches irrevocable disrepair. Do not purposely go into a relationship, choosing to build upon lies, because it will take root, it will grow, and it will eventually produce death within that relationship. No one goes into a relationship expecting to feel unimportant or devalued, yet it happens. It happens even without the lies, so don't choose to deal damage that you can opt out of from the beginning.

So how do we mitigate the common occurrence of the entitlement of being right and keep the emotional hijack from causing damage?

Simply do damage control up front. Take that breath, move out of that physical lock up, and ask them why they feel that way or why they think that is so – something to get them talking and you thinking. Once they start talking, do not cue up your response, but listen! If you are so focused on what you will say in defense of the accusation, you are just buying time to be even more right in your reaction, you are not doing damage control at that point, you are loading up with more explosives! Don't do it! Instead, take a moment to listen to what is really going on with that other individual. What happened to make them feel unimportant and devalued? Did you have a role in this – intentional or not? Is there a way that you can demonstrate the other party's importance and value by a gesture or a soft response? How can you truthfully demonstrate personal responsibility to show that you value the other person in this relationship more than just being right? Aren't they worth more than just being right?

You must have right thinking to start, before you can begin to demonstrate personal responsibility. In order to develop this right thinking, you must identify your core values and be aware when these are being trampled by another – intentionally or unintentionally, it all feels the same. You can be emotionally hijacked by the accusation and you can be emotionally hijacked by observing what you perceive to be an affront to one of your core values. So if a core value is hard work, where you view yourself as a hard worker and feel that others should do the same (your expectation), be aware that you can easily become emotionally hijacked when you believe that someone is accusing you of not being a hard worker or if that same person is displaying a lack of hard work on the team. It works both ways.

This is why it is so important to figure out where these hot spots are within your expectations. What are your core values? I'm not referring to the generic values of family, work, home, but, like I said before, the ones that, when you are accused of going against them, it sends you to the moon faster than anything else! I personally have core values that can get me going, like hard work and professionalism, but I also have a personality that, I am aware, lends itself towards being laid back and sometimes less than professional, so I don't take those as personal when confronted. For me, a main core value is my integrity. If someone accuses me of not having integrity, whether they meant to or not, it gets me seeing red in no time! It doesn't matter who it is, if they call my integrity into question, I will pounce on the opportunity to prove them wrong and shut them down – they surely know then that they hit a nerve! They may have no idea what nerve they hit, but they are certain when it's all over that they just did something that really ticked me off.

I am not the violent type, never have been, never will be, because it doesn't look right on me – in fact it looks really odd on me and quite silly. I have always been the type to become very silent when angry and display that anger through my non-verbal cues and an unnervingly quiet and low tone. I also find it very easy to pick the most deadly of phrases that I know will cut to the quick, offending the core value of my "opponent" for a one move, one kill exchange of words. Not a good tactic, I know. This produces a very efficient and effective kill rate for relationships, which is exactly the opposite of what I want, so I have to be very aware and extremely intentional about what I do and what I say when my core value of integrity is offended.

Once the offense does come, I stop for a moment and the first thought that goes through my head is almost always in preparation to be right, until the second thought saunters into my head – wait, are they right? This causes me to consider if there is any merit to what they are saying, are they way off base or was there something that I said or did to give them reason to question my integrity? Are they speaking truth? Did I fail to display my integrity in the best way possible? What was my personal responsibility? If there is a shred of truth to this, whether intentional or unintentional upon my part, I begin to listen to what the other person is saying, trying to decipher how I made them feel unimportant and devalued through my conduct. I may have thought about taking a certain action to save time, so I felt that it was in the best interest of everyone involved, but when I took that action, it impacted another in a negative way that I did not consider. I have often come to a peaceable resolution by apologizing, which doesn't always feel great, thereby getting the result of a healthy relationship.

Jim had quietly packed up all of the garbage into the back of his truck. I couldn't take it anymore, so I broke the silence. "Boy, that was tense, hunh?"

"Naw. She's a good woman, she just gets into a mode of taking care of business that her mind goes a million miles a minute and tries to do it all. Once she realizes all that needs to be done, she gets stressed out and then comes to me for help, although I don't always handle it the best. I know that she has the best intentions, but sometimes I get my mind on something and it is hard for me to just drop what I am doing to help her. I don't fault her for it and I wish I didn't get so frustrated, because she has a heart of gold." Jim trailed off thoughtfully.

"Well that's for sure! And she can cook too! So it's pizza tonight, hunh?" I tried to change the subject to ease tension.

"Yeah! Oh man, does she make a mean pizza! I think I smelled bacon in the oven when I went inside and I saw that she had pepperoni, mushrooms, peppers, onions, and black olives cut up and ready to be put on the pizza!" Jim started to drool a little.

"So we'd better get the dump run done, pick up the pizza sauce, and get back to the house quick! I'm hungry!" I said as my stomach growled, echoing the sentiment.

We got to the dump, threw the bags into the hopper, and took the recyclables into the open bay. Jim started to chat with the transfer station attendant, who was a pretty nice guy, but extremely talkative! Jim sure knew how to make people feel important and valued, especially when he was engaged in conversation, because he is adept at picking up on other people's non-verbal cues, so the conversation never lags. However, that's the other issue, is that the conversation never lags and next thing I know, we've been at the transfer station for over 30 minutes! I coughed loudly, which caught Jim's attention. I gestured to my watch and he politely excused himself from the conversation, knowing that Kay was waiting for the pizza sauce.

Jim checked his cell phone and saw a message from Kay, "Where are you?!?!?!!!???"

"Shoot! I totally got caught up in that conversation! Maybe I'll wait to text her back." Jim reasoned.

I shot him a sideways glance, knowing that waiting would just make it worse. Jim began to panic, "Yeah, I know. Shoot! Shoot! Shoot! She is going to be ticked! So what do I say? I know that she is waiting!"

"Maybe you should tell her the truth?" I offered.

"What, that I got talking to the guy at the transfer station? I don't know. She won't feel too wonderful that he is taking up her time!" Jim shook his head.

Jim was right. Kay wouldn't feel too wonderful about Jim giving his time away to the transfer station attendant, because he knew that she valued his time, but she sometimes felt like he didn't value her time – it all came down to her core value of support. Kay had everything ready for the pizza and Jim was only supposed to be 15 minutes at most to dump off the garbage at the transfer station, go to the store, pick up pizza sauce, and then bring it back home – why would he be 30 minutes? Jim wasn't thinking about Kay when he started talking to the transfer station attendant, he was thinking that this guy was having a rough day, because a transfer station patron had just given the attendant a really rough time about dropping off brush. This particular patron had thought that the brush pile drop off area would be easy to get to, but instead, it had to be unlocked, taking longer than expected, so the guy let loose on the attendant, yelling like a fool. Jim saw an opportunity to make things a little less horrible for the attendant, so he took that it, forgetting the time constraints he was under.

By the time that Jim had realized what had happened, the damage was already done. At no point did Jim intend for this to happen, but the fact of the matter was that he did it, whether he meant to or not. Motive does not change the fact that it was now 30 minutes later and he could not change that. Jim now had a choice to get results or to be right – lying is not an option because Kay is important to him and he values her trust and their relationship. Jim knows that she is upset because of the tone of the text, but does not know the full extent, so he is now in the beginning stages of an emotional hijack. Jim prepares himself and says, "Well, might as well tell her what really happened and throw myself on the mercies of the court!"

"Good call." I chimed.

Jim sent the following text: "Hun, I'm so sorry that I'm not back yet. There was a real jerk yelling at the transfer station guy, so I wanted to make him feel better and the conversation went on longer than I planned. I'm heading to the store now to get the pizza sauce and I will make it up to you when I get home." Jim took a deep breath as he pushed send and waited.

It seemed like an eternity for Kay's response to arrive. We were heading into the store, when a text alert popped up on his phone. Jim paused, opened up his phone, and as he read it, a smile came across his face. "Man oh man! Do I love that woman!" Jim exclaimed.

"What did it say?" I pried.

"Just that I would have to save the making it up for after I change our youngest' s diaper. Also to pick up chocolate." Jim smirked.

"Was that all? It seems like you got off unscathed!" I asked disbelievingly.

"No, that wasn't all, but the rest is for my eyes only." Jim's smirk grew into a huge grin.

"Okay, okay. Let's just get the pizza sauce. And don't forget the chocolate!" I added as we went into the store.

Exercise:

1. Take your previous list of 6 individuals from Chapter 2's exercise. Look at the list again and review what you had written. You should be getting used to this.

2. Look at each of these interactions - what made you feel unimportant and devalued. Try to describe it in one word in each case. Is it hard work, integrity, autonomy, responsibility, support, or something else?

3. Look at each of these interactions - what made the other person feel unimportant and devalued in each case? Again, try to describe it in one word.

4. What were the specific observable behaviors (actions) in each case that the other person could observe (see and hear) you do? How did you emotionally hijack them?

5. What were the specific observable behaviors (actions) in each case that you could observe (see and hear) the other person do? How did they emotionally hijack you?

6. Was there any truth to each side? Is there something to consider that you did, intentionally or unintentionally that led towards the emotional hijack?

7. Thinking about this now, what could you have done differently (only you, not the other person – personal responsibility) to ensure that you did not accuse the other person of going against their core value? Be sure to use specific observable behaviors.

8. Were you only attempting to be right or did you attempt to get results? At any point, did you "listen" only to find a way to be right and do further damage? What was the result of that?

9. Is it possible that the other person sees things differently than you do in this situation? If you shared this with them, what do you think they would say?

Building on previous lessons learned, we take personal responsibility to demonstrate importance and value to the other person, thereby exhibiting right thinking/feeling/action and getting the results we want. The way to start with right thinking is to ensure that we know our core values, aka, what sends us off the deep end faster than anything else. Once we are aware of these core values, we must ask if there is any truth to another's accusation of going against our core values, along with intentionally seeking out ways to get the result of a healthy relationship. Did we emotionally hijack the other person (intentionally or unintentionally) and what can we do to repair the damage that has been done? Lying is never an option. There are times that these things will only take you so far, especially if the way that you see things and the world around you is the result of viewing these situations through a very different lens. My next important finding was to consider the way you view the world around you and determine the impact that has on your relationships.

Chapter 4

"Jessica, it's all right!" Kay exclaimed.

"No Mom! It's not all right! It's not fair! You're being mean to me!" Jessica stamped her foot on the ground.

Kay took a breath, "Jessica, I have told you that you cannot have chocolate for breakfast, because after you eat it, you will still be hungry, which is why I have made you some eggs. Now why don't you sit down and eat your eggs, then after a little bit we can talk about some chocolate."

"I don't want eggs! They're gross!" Jessica had her head down, but looked up at her mother through a furrowed brow.

"I have fixed your eggs the same way that I did yesterday, complete with barbeque sauce on the side. No go sit down and eat your eggs and then I will think about giving you some chocolate." Kay attempted to reason.

Jessica decided to switch up her game, where the pouting wasn't working. "So can I have some chocolate with my eggs?"

Kay laughed, because of the ingenious tactic Jessica employed, "No, silly, you can't have chocolate with your eggs."

"Why not?" Jessica asked with a sad puppy dog face and a shrug of the shoulders.

"Because I have already told you what you needed to do if you want chocolate." Kay responded.

"Why not?" Jessica resorted to a battle of attrition of the will.

"Asked and answered." Kay volleyed back the tried and true default of her parenting arsenal, where the child had asked and she had answered, end of story.

Jessica was not deterred. "Why not?"

"Asked and answered." Kay sung back.

"Oh fine." Jessica climbed up into the pub chair and took the smallest bit of egg that she could nibble and declared, "I'm full!"

Kay walked over and glanced into the bowl. "Nice try. How about you at least eat this half and then we'll talk about chocolate." Kay scraped half of the eggs to one side of the bowl and gestured at them with the fork.

"T-chaw. Fine!" Jessica obliged with exasperation. Jessica began eating the eggs, giving a running tally of each bite that she had taken, but mixing the two halves together, while humming a song. "Look mumma, I did it!"

Kay looked into the bowl and sure enough, Jessica had finished not only the half that she had agreed to eat, but also a large portion of the other half as well. Kay smiled and stated, "Now that you are done, let's go look at getting some chocolate."

Kay doled out three colorfully shelled chocolates as Jessica squealed in delight. Kay smirked as she watched Jessica count out the number of candies and eat each one deliberately.

This is what our view of the world, our perspective, can do to a normally functioning relationship – add opposition and challenges. Jessica is a sweet child, with a sincere love of chocolate, but Kay knows that chocolate is only beneficial in small amounts, so as to ensure the proper growth and development of the child that she loves. However, when Kay refuses to give out chocolate before breakfast, Jessica looks at her mother as the cruelest person on the face of the earth! "Why not?!" is the choice repetition, employed to erode even the strongest constitution and bring even the utmost of parenting skills to a grinding halt. The issue here is that the "grinding halt" is usually accompanied by undesirable results. Either the parent raises their voice, resulting in everyone being upset or the child succeeds with the badgering request, resulting in the parent feeling defeated– this is not good for either party, either way!

The choice that Kay has made was one of intention, where it was her intention to demonstrate that her daughter's health was important and valued, as well as the intention to fulfill the desire to treat her daughter for complying. Jessica only saw that her mother was withholding something that she wanted, when she exclaimed that her mother was mean. So was Jessica emotionally hijacked? Maybe, but most likely she was not. Kids are remarkable at turning the annoying behaviors on and off like a light switch! Kids also deploy an unequivocal ability to push your buttons that they innately seem to locate with some sort of kid sonar. Children can emotionally hijack a parent faster than most! We live in a society where we expect that everyone will relate to one another by a certain set of reciprocal rules; you scratch my back, I'll scratch yours. We are courteous and patient, just trying to live peaceably, day in and day out. Not children though.

Children are masters at getting what they want, when they want it, because they have a very strong expectation of getting what they want and no shame in getting it. A child does not care who is around them in the store. If they can't have what they want, everyone will know it then and there! The tantrum ensues and the parent gets emotionally hijacked by a half sized human. They either begin to fight with the child through failed attempts at reason, they freeze up out of frustrated embarrassment, or they take to flight from the tantrum by giving into the pint sized dictator's demands. Children are masters at being self-centered and not giving a hoot what other people think in the moment, even if the other people are getting emotionally hijacked; they just want what they want. This is a child's view of the world and relationships.

The parent's view is that they have a mile long list of items that they need to purchase, get out of the store as quick as possible, and move onto the next chore on their lengthy to-do list. The unsuspecting parent enters the store, bordering on an emotional hijack, due to pre-elevated stress levels, when they walk past the advertised toy surprise in a box of sugar filled cereal, which catches the eye of the child. The child then makes their list of demands. The parent may immediately give in, for fear of negotiations breaking down, but the parent remembers that this only temporarily diffuses the situation and causes the demands to snowball out of control; so they say no. The child then ramps up the volume of the demand, still maintaining a level of control, so that the full manipulation can have a much greater effect; the parent retains their intestinal fortitude and firmly repeats NO. This is unacceptable from the child's point of view and it is time for the show! Pull back the curtain, grab your popcorn, and away with the tantrum! Whether we have kids or not, we have all seen this happen, yet we are often remiss in acknowledging the role that perspective plays.

The child's perspective is to serve their self, and no one else! The parent's perspective is to provide for the family and ensure that there is enough food in the house, not to solely meet the child's demands. When these two perspectives do not match up, then we have a conflict. The child's expectations are different based off of their self-centered perspective. It's not that they don't care for their parent or the other individuals in the household, but when self is in first place you, as the parent, have to make ready for battle. The parent's perspective is putting others first, which is why the cart is not overflowing with chocolate, ramen, and wine, but wholesome and nutritious food (with some of the chocolate thrown in here and there). Our perspectives will cause us to build up our expectations in such a manner that we deem certain components or our interactions as necessary and optimal. Based on previous interactions and biases some things will be viewed as tangible or anticipated, or, conversely, cause us to become hesitant and cautious. Perspectives play a large role in determining our expectations, so much so, that we should not neglect where they stem from.

Our perspective is borne out of the way that we view the world, and how we make sense of it all. As we grow and mature, we take the information that is available to us and begin to put the pieces together in a way that works for our mental image. If we have never used a telephone, watched a sitcom on a television, or streamed a movie on demand, then we have no perspective on how these things would impact someone's life – we don't know what we're missing. If your first experience binge watch a series was with a significant other and you both found it to be enjoyable, then your perspective of this activity takes on meaning that this is a positive experience. However, if your first involvement in binge watching is that your significant other favors spending time binge watching a series and ignoring you, then your perspective on that activity may cause you to become a little bit embittered. Perspective is formulated from our interaction with the world around us and can lead to very skewed ideas on how the world works, forming expectations that may be a little off.

We only have so many sources of information available to us in a given geographic region and even though the World Wide Web has expanded our accessibility quite a bit, experience will always be a much more influential teacher than any other source of information. Someone that almost drowned as a child will have a very real and strong fear of water, even if they are in a shallow 6' pool – if they can't easily touch the bottom, then forget it! They aren't even putting on their bathing suit! The same goes for a person that was bit by a dog, or fell from a height, or was involved in a motorcycle accident – these are all very real incidents that can change someone's perspective forever. Right or wrong, the stronger the experience, the stronger our perspective will become towards that person, place, or thing, causing us to act irrationally and get emotionally hijacked, even when the logical side of our brain tells us that we know better.

A perfect example of this irrational emotional hijack is the old trick of guessing what is in the box. The person walks up to a covered box and has to guess its contents. The only issue is that they do not know what is in the covered box, so the trepidation and fear begin to raise their stress levels and they are now primed for the fight, flight, or freeze response! They slowly reach their hand into the covered box and quickly withdraw it, even though they haven't felt anything yet. For some odd reason, they choose to slowly creep their hand back into the box and feel something slimy, round, and moving! Oh my goodness! They have no idea what that was, but it was alive! Ahhhh! This is just their irrational emotional hijack taking over, skewing their perspective, enticing them to believe that they just felt something slimy, round, and moving. The truth is that it was just a bowl of peeled grapes. Definitely not moving and definitely not alive.

You may have seen viral videos of grown men, blindfolded, screaming in terror as their hand was guided down into an open top plexi glass box, only to shriek when their hand brushed up against a big eyed, furry stuffed animal. This is hilarious to us, yet terrifying to them, all because of the difference in perspective – a simple piece of cloth restricting certain bits of key information can quickly ruin our bravery. Once the blindfold is removed, the grown man then begins to posture, feeling foolish for having shrieked, and tries to reclaim some of the machismo that has been reduced to the level of cute and cuddly that is sitting inside the open top plexi glass box. Once we are in a place to have things properly revealed to us, then we will begin to change our perspective, but not a moment sooner – even if our perspective is absolutely wrong.

Perspectives direct our expectations, our expectations directly influence our thoughts, which will turn into feelings, feelings turn into actions, actions into conduct, and conduct into reputation. This is why understanding that not all people have the same perspective is so important, because if we all had the same perspective, then expectations, thoughts, feelings, actions, conduct, and reputation would all sync up into a very predictive and homogeneous world. Our differences account for so many wonderful things in this world, but they also account for a lot of confusion and conflict, which is why we must first understand our own perspectives and how they form our expectations, thereby impacting our thoughts. So how do our perspectives form in the first place?

When we experience something, we take in the information around us, we use our senses to make meaning out of the situation, which generates an emotional response and we link a memory to it. These memories can be extremely strong and influential in determining how our perspectives form, to the extent that a strong experience will forever trigger a memory of that experience for better or worse. Think of a scent that you really enjoy. Is it fresh cut grass or the saltiness of the beach? How about newly laid asphalt or gasoline? Maybe even lilacs in bloom or a cup of strong Columbian coffee? Can you think of a scent that is enjoyable? What about one that brings back a feeling of romance or dread or sorrow? There is probably a memory attached to that scent that will send you to that memory every time.

I remember working at the production facility and walking out into the yard for my pre-shift inspection It was the quietest time of the day, because none of the other workers had arrived yet for their shift. The yard sat by a river, which had a crisp scent of waking up, that wafted together with the smell of hydraulic fluid and diesel fuel that came from the containers in the refueling station located on the other side of the yard. I would purposely walk by the refueling station as the sun peeked up over the embankment, feeling the cold crisp morning mixing with the warmth of the sun; these scents locked to the memory of my process of mentally preparing for the day. This was such a consistent event that even now, when I am walking from my vehicle to my office in the morning certain smells and senses can take me right back there. I can smell the scent of the river on my left mixing with the exhaust from the vehicles passing by on my right, the cold crisp morning offset by the sun's warmth brings me back to the quiet mornings at the processing facility, even though I work for a completely different company in a completely different town. This link is strong.

This link is so strong, in fact, that it will play a large role in forming your perspectives in life and your core values. If you find that you are offended easily or offend others easily, then it may have something to do with your perspective. Have you ever wondered how someone could do something so weird, wacky, horrible, or crazy? That's because your perspective is vastly different from that other weird, wacky, horrible, or crazy individual. If your perspective is different enough from others around you, then your expectations will be as well. These expectations will then translate down through thoughts/feelings/actions, creating a difficult environment, in which, it is difficult for healthy relationships to thrive. Remember that your perspectives will directly influence your expectations, so if you consistently have unmet expectations, then you are consistently primed for an emotional hijack the majority of the time.

There are societal norms that every person should pick up on, to assist in forming memories that cement what society deems appropriate and what is not appropriate. If we miss these cues at various stages in our development, then we will remain as a self-serving child, like the one that we met at the beginning of the chapter; impetuous, entitled, and demanding. How many times have we heard of a young boy constantly running his mouth, until one day, one of the other kids has enough of this aggravation and punches the boy in the face? I am not advocating for frustration to beget violence. However, in this interaction, the loud mouthed boy learns to temper what he says, because in the future someone may become fed up with his comments, resulting in a similar physical pain. The perspective of the young boy that was constantly running his mouth has now changed from speaking without thinking, to considering what impact this will have on others before he opens his mouth. Now, this young boy is taking an interest in other's non-verbal cues to see if those around him are getting fed up with his comments or if he can go just a little further with his prodding. His perspective has changed permanently, to the extent that he will no longer assume that everyone shares his sense of humor. This experience is a very strong teacher of a lesson that will never be forgotten!

What strong experiences have you had that permanently changed your perspective, for better or worse? Do these bias your decisions or judgements? What effect do these strong experiences have on your expectations that have formed? Have these expectations caused you trouble or led you towards success? What do you attribute this trouble or success to in your life? Hopefully you are thinking of answers to these questions, to jump start the reflective nature that I am hoping to spur on in you. It might seem quite overwhelming at first, but just take one step at a time or one situation at a time. If you have an interaction that went well, ask yourself why. The same goes for an interaction that didn't go well, again, ask yourself why. Use the outline that we have for each and every interaction. At first it is a bit overwhelming, but eventually you will become very adept at this reflective skill.

It was late one night in central Florida, when Bobby and I were walking back to our apartment, reveling in the night's festivities at the chemical free club, from which, we had just emerged. Bobby looked over at me and said, "Whoo! That was quite something! But I'm beat and we need to find a cab!"

"Good idea. Maybe around the corner on Church Street?" I suggested.

Church Street was only a couple of blocks away, so we decided to walk over and noticed that it was early morning. "No way! It's 3:30! I hope there's a cab down here!" I looked nervously at Bobby.

"Okay. So here's the plan. I'll head that way and you go that way and if either one of us find a cab, we meet back here in 10 minutes with said cab." Bobby always had a plan.

So we parted ways and I began to walk down the street, when I ran into a homeless gentleman. "Spare some change?" he asked with an outstretched hand, a little closer than I liked.

I knew that I needed five dollars to pay for my portion of the cab fare, but I did have three one's in my pocket, so I pulled them out, saying, "This is all I have mister."

It was almost as if he could see through me and he could tell that I had more, which worried me a little bit, because I knew better than to be out in this part of central Florida at 3:30 in the morning. "Hey kid, why don't you walk with me? This ain't the best place for a young man like you to be by yourself. You need a cab?" He asked, getting closer.

I stood up a little straighter, looked him in the eye, trying not to be the victim, and deepening my voice, I replied, "Yeah I am. My buddy is back there and we're looking for a cab."

"Oh he is, is he?" The man asked, which rattled me to my core.

I knew that I was in a potentially bad situation, so I did the best thing that I could think to do at the moment. "Yeah, we're going to meet back up over there in about 10 minutes with a cab and I have to be back there because he has all the cash." I was a wimp!

"Well, no need to get all worked up my friend! I'm just saying that a young guy like you ain't in the right part of town at this time of night. That's all." He began to talk and

I softened as I realized that he meant no ill will, as we conversed.

Another homeless man asked for change and the gentlemen that I was with piped up, "He ain't got no money, now leave him alone!" I was relieved for the moment.

I became a little more comfortable as we talked, so I asked him, "You seem like a really nice guy, do you mind if I ask you how in the world you ended up here?" feeling rude, I almost instantly regretted what I had just asked.

"You want to know my story? Shoot. No one ever asks my story. Well young man, I'll keep it short, because you have to meet your friend to catch a cab." And he proceeded to tell me how he ended up on the street.

The gentleman explained that he had been gainfully employed in his youth, but due to travel he began to drink more than he should and eventually his wife and kids left him. He continued to try to work, but the drinking became too much and he soon lost his job, which caused him to drink even more. Both of his parents had passed away and he went to his sister for help, but she couldn't help him for long, because she had problems of her own, so eventually he ended up on the streets. He had tried some of the local shelters, in an attempt to get cleaned up to apply for a job, but when employers looked at his resume, they would always question his employment gap and he would eventually lose out on the position. "Do you know how hard it is to get a job, when you can't get a shower, or have a place to put your stuff where someone else won't steal it while you at work? Shoot man! Don't ever do what I did young man! Stay away from drugs and alcohol, they will ruin you!" he shook his head.

"I am so sorry. Is there something that I can do?" I asked, not really having anything to offer.

"You want to help me?" he paused reflectively. "Naw. I'm good. You already did help me by actually listening to me. It's been so long since someone would talk to me, like a human being!" He smiled.

"Well it was easy to listen! You have quite the story!" I said with a waver in my voice.

"Son, just keep doing what you doing and don't get wrapped up in the stuff that I did. Learn from other's mistakes and just try to make people's days brighter. You don't need to bring them the world, just show them you care and that's enough." His smile outshone the streetlights.

Just then a cab pulled up a couple hundred yards away and Bobby's head popped out. "Come on! Let's go! Or are you walkin?" he yelled.

"Thank you so much! Maybe I'll see you again next week?" I hoped.

"Maybe, my friend. You take care and God bless." He waved as I ran toward the cab.

I have not forgotten that interaction and it has irrevocably changed my perspective on the homeless, from potentially dangerous individuals that were just looking for money, to where I can see that they are people that are in a tough situation. Most still have a sense of pride and don't want pity, just kindness and compassion. Just show them that you care in some way and that's enough. It stuck with me. I can still remember every detail. The most important detail is that he had changed my perspective, so now showing someone that I care is central to my interactions – how can I show someone that they are important and I value them? It's not always easy, but at least I'm trying each and every day to tap into that perspective that has stemmed from very wise advice. Caring and kindness go so much further than money. Money comes and goes without much attachment and temporarily quells our disdain for our selfish nature. But caring and kindness takes something more, something from within our soles that we have to stop and recognize what they do for others and ourselves – they change perspectives. Changed perspectives will lead to changed expectations, this will lead to changed thoughts, feelings, and actions, which will lead to changed conduct, and ultimately changed reputations. How would you like to change?

Exercise:

1. Take your previous list of 6 interactions from Chapter 3's exercise. The details on the list should be building and becoming quite deep, so pick 4 out of the 6 to go further. (or keep all 6, it's up to you.)

2. What was your perspective on the interaction? Was it different than the other person's perspective? Were the reactions different? Why or why not?

3. If you both saw the same thing and heard the same thing, then why would there be differences in the reaction? What made your perspectives and expectations different? Try looking back on what made each of you feel unimportant and devalued.

4. How did this lead towards an emotional hijack? Did perspective and expectation play a small or large role in the emotional hijack? What is the reasoning behind this?

5. What role did your perspective and expectations play in the development or internalization of your core values? An emotional hijack is a result of an accusation of going against core values, so which of these core values were involved?

6. Do you believe that your observation of the interaction was 100% accurate? Or did you filter information through your perspective? Did you cater to your own expectations? Was there truth to any of the accusations of going against your core values?

7. If you look at the interaction, what was the catalyst (the thing that started it all)? What were your thoughts at that moment? Were these thoughts based in truth? Was there something you could have done to mitigate the conflict? If so, what? How would this have altered the outcome?

Your perspective can change - hopefully not from a traumatic event, but from a choice. A choice to see things differently in order to maintain healthy relationships, not just get what you can out of people and discard them when their usefulness has been wrung out. We are not children anymore, so self-serving and manipulative behavior should not be in your relationship building repertoire, but a desire to consider other's needs before your own, seeking to demonstrate importance and value to those around us. Ultimately, this personal responsibility rests upon us, to live peaceably, even when others choose not to do so.

My next important finding was to consider that it is not easy to strive to live peaceably, because our perspectives can leave us unable to form healthy relationships. I then had to answer another question: are we stuck this way or can we learn to change? If we can learn to change, then there must be a gold standard. There must be some sort of template in forming healthy relationships that we can look to as an example, but who, if anyone, has done it perfectly? Who could be our template, by which, we can learn to change?

Chapter 5

"I just don't know what to do. Meeting someone at a bar is not an option. There's no one that I have met up until now, just going about my life. I mean, I get up, get the kids ready for school, go to work, then come home, get the kids dinner, then bath and bed. Usually I'm sitting on the couch by myself until I think I can fall asleep, only to toss and turn all night and wake up the next day to do it all again. Maybe it's better to just accept single parenthood as my life." Charlie shrunk down into his chair even further.

"Charlie, man, come on. It's not that bad. I mean, what have you tried so far?" John asked in a nonchalant tone.

"I don't know. I've really only been working and haven't been paying all that much attention to dating. I think it's all for the best, you know, just to focus on the kids right now. They need me more than I need a relationship… that would only make things way too complicated." Charlie was ready to admit defeat.

John shook his head, "Okay then. You and your kids are on a plane, going on vacation. All of a sudden, the plane loses cabin pressure and the masks drop down from the ceiling. What do you do first?"

"I put them on my kids of course." Charlie looked shocked at the question.

"That's not what they tell you to do though. They tell you specifically to put the mask on yourself, before you help others. That way you don't become another victim, along with the other people that are having trouble with their mask. Your kids won't be able to help you. If you don't get yourself squared around to begin with, you will be in no shape to help them when they really need you - when they need to exit the plane." John reasoned.

"I guess I never thought of it like that." Charlie was now pondering John's diatribe.

"If you don't make sure that you are in a good space, then how will you have the ability to care for those that really need you? Right now you're making it work, but eventually you need to do something to course correct, my friend. I'm not saying go out and get married tomorrow, but it's not good that you're alone. There's no way you're going to get back with the kids' mother, right?" John was really hitting a nerve.

"Nope. That ship has sailed." Charlie looked at the floor.

"Well, at least you know that. Right? So you need to look at this whole thing differently. You had a relationship that didn't work out. You're human. It happens. It's been a while and things are not going to be mended. You've accepted that, so now it's time to move on. Or is it?" John's question prompted some reflection.

"Well. I'm just not sure. What if I get it wrong? There's more than just my feelings at stake here. I have to consider the kids." Charlie was trying to weasel out of answering.

"Of course there's more at stake, so don't be stupid about it! You know what you should and shouldn't do! Just don't get physical until you know the person and even then, be sure to guard your heart. You know this!" John reminded Charlie.

"Oh, I'm not ready to get physical by any means!" Charlie quickly added.

John raised an eyebrow and laughed, then grabbed Charlie's wrist. "What are you doing?" Charlie asked, confused by John's actions.

"Just making sure you still have a pulse." John laughed at his own quick wit.

"Hilarious." Charlie was less than impressed, but had to admit that John was right. Charlie was still alive and the physical side of a relationship was something that he would eventually be ready for.

"Look, all I'm saying is to take it slow, don't get physical, but at least put yourself out there. I mean, it's been a while and being single is obviously taking a toll on you. It's not good for you and it's not good for the kids. You are obviously not getting back together with their mother, so at least live your life man. Who knows what will happen?" John was trying to be encouraging as possible.

"That's just it. Who knows what will happen." Charlie looked at John with a hard gaze.

"Hey, if you're not ready that's fine, but don't sit around all mopey just because you had a relationship that didn't end in sunshine and roses. This does not have to be what makes you. You know the truth and you know how you should conduct yourself. I would trust that you will do this thing right. Take every thought captive and only let what is right and honorable become your actions. Besides, you are a miserable single person…. and a real downer… and I want the fun Charlie back! Because we both know that it's all about me." John laughed again.

Charlie shook his head and began to laugh, "It is all about you. So I need to move on, so your life can get back to normal."

"Yeah, ya know, if you could just build a bridge and get over it that would be great." John slapped Charlie on the back.

"I'll get right on it. Are we doing lunch?" Charlie asked.

"Of course! I'll fly, you buy?" John wasn't asking, but more so implying.

"It's the least I can do for you listening to me whine for the last hour!" Charlie cracked a smile and chucked.

How often do we have an interaction (or relationship) that doesn't go so well and we allow it to change our perspective in ways that are damaging to our ability to maintain other healthy relationships? Sometimes we have an interaction that wounds us so deeply that we think we may never recover and, as a result, have significant difficulty in trusting others. This wound is deep, causing a shift in our core values, leading us towards a state of heightened stress, where we are primed for an emotional hijack at any moment. This state is not good for anyone. This perspective is not good for anyone. So how do we get our perspective back to where it was before this damaging relationship?

The first step is being aware and acknowledging the significant impact that this damage has had on your perspective. This realization should cue you into the change that your expectations have undergone, in regards to what you are comfortable with in your relationships. From that point forward these new expectations will impact your thinking. For example, if you are now a more suspicious person, then you will be waiting for the moment that the new person lies, cheats, or in some other way hurts you. This is not rational, because this new person did not commit the original offense! However, your perspective has been so altered by the damaging interaction that your heightened stress keeps you just below the level of a constant emotional hijack. Your suspicious thoughts then turn into suspicious feelings. These feelings then develop into suspicious actions, followed by suspicious conduct, and eventually leading the new person coming to know you as a suspicious person. This will almost always lead towards conflict, where this constant suspicion devalues others through constant distrust – a healthy relationship cannot thrive in this environment.

Think back to Chapter 1. I am not keen on just being aware. I feel the need to actually do something about this and make some sort of change. It is important to identify another individual (or individuals) who will support you through this journey of healing and realignment of your perspective. You cannot do this alone. There is safety in a multitude of counselors, so surround yourself with people that you know that you can trust. That way when the suspicion arises, it is mitigated by what you know – you think about the fact that these are trustworthy people that have no reason to betray you. Having a safety net of supportive people that you can be vulnerable with is key to getting things back on track. They will be there to comfort, encourage, and sometimes push you towards where you need to go. These people have only one stake in the course of things, to see you get to a good place, so that you can maintain healthy relationships once again.

In order to wright your perspective, you have to consider what led to the demise of the previous relationship. Ultimately no one is ever the innocent party – you both played a part, no matter how minor. It didn't work between the two of you. So, take personal responsibility as you think about that relationship and all of the interactions you both shared. What were you thinking and feeling? How did you display that? What were they thinking and feeling? How did they display that? Did you each have different expectations of the other and yourselves? Were your perspectives similar or different of what was permissible and what was not allowed within a relationship? Was there something that you could have done differently to possibly get results instead of being right? What did they do to emotionally hijack you (intentionally or unintentionally)? What did you do that emotionally hijacked them (intentionally or unintentionally)? Were there a lot of little things that accumulated into an emotional hijack? All of these components will lead you to figuring out where things went sideways, so as to reflect and grow.

Now that you have reflected on the personal responsibility that you had in the demise of this relationship, minimally or majorly, let's note it and move on, because staying there and feeling bad does no one any good. Learn from it. Let it change your perspective. Let it change your expectations in such a way that it will remind you in future interactions that you have a choice to live peaceably. You have a choice to take your thoughts captive before they turn into feelings, actions, conduct, and a reputation. You have a choice. Say it out loud. "I have a choice." If you are going to choose to change your perspective, your expectations, your thinking, your feelings, your actions, your conduct, and your reputation then you are ready to start towards a path of having healthy relationships; despite what goes on around you or what happens to you. You have a choice to be emotionally hijacked or to take that moment to be true to your core values and demonstrate importance and value to that other individual, regardless of their actions.

Treating others in a manner that is consistent with your core values is not accomplished by casual efforts, but by an intentional focus when conflict does arise. You will have a choice to make, so what is it going to be? Is this choice a monumental test that you seem to fail, over and over? Maybe, despite all of your efforts, it just isn't enough and you can't seem to get away from the emotional hijack. Striving to live peaceably may be an insurmountable task that you just can't seem to make happen as often as you would like. Something to remember – none of us are perfect and we all struggle with this. We struggle no matter what kind of relationship we are in, no matter who is involved, no matter what we choose to do, and no matter how hard we try. We are all flawed and so are our perspectives. However, there is a way to get closer to failing less and less with every opportunity that comes our way – learn from someone who did it right, who never missed the mark of perfection.

Perfection is a funny thing. Just when we think we have achieved it, we learn that we have so much further to go. There is no way to know someone else's every thought and feeling, therefore, we cannot perfectly predict the optimal response that we should offer in any given situation. We cannot see into the deepest part of a person's heart or mind, neither can they see into ours, which is why we rely on non-verbal cues and tone. The problem is that this leaves us wanting, because we don't always get it right. This is why our perspective kicks in and our expectations fill the gaps of what we can't see or know. Sometimes we get it right, sometimes we don't, but ultimately we try to navigate the best that we can to live peaceably through different types of relationships. Our choice of directions are determined by what kind of relationships we are investing in and how the interactions play out; relationships can be take only, the give and take of friends, the give and take of intimacy, and give only.

In relationships, there is something called emotional capital, where you have a certain amount of emotional capacity to invest in another individual. If the relationship is healthy, then the emotional capital will grow, causing you to invest more in the relationship, creating a stronger tie. If the relationship is not healthy, then the emotional capital will eventually be depleted, causing the relationship to eventually die, thereby severing the tie between you and the other individual. Think about the relationships that you have now, reflecting on some of the relationships that you have listed in the previous chapter's exercises, as I describe the various types of emotional investment you can make.

A take only relationship is where one person will take, without fulfilling the reasonable expectation of giving back to the relationship. This interaction will leave you feeling unimportant and devalued every time. The problem is that you may not realize that it is a take only relationship until the taker has absorbed significant emotional capital, leaving you with a choice to either sever the relationship or continuing to borrow emotional capital from other relationships. Your borrowed emotional capital will be leached from other otherwise healthy relationships to fulfill this unrelenting expectation of the taker; this will cause you to become a taker within your other relationships. Your perspective will become that of keeping this take only relationship going, so your expectation will be to continue to pour in the emotional capital.

Your lack of resource will drive thoughts of inadequacy because you cannot keep up with the high demands of the necessary emotional investment. Soon follow the feelings of inadequacy, driving you to feel like if you could only give a little more, that you would be important enough for the other individual to value your efforts. These feelings direct your actions, so much so that you drain all of your emotional capital into this unhealthy relationship. Eventually your conduct becomes such that everything revolves around this unhealthy relationship and you begin to drain emotional capital from your healthy relationships; gaining a reputation for being a taker as well. It is at this point that you are highly susceptible to living in a constant state of emotional hijack and it is not until you sever this relationship that you will begin to realize the impact that it had on your perspective, expectations, thoughts, feelings, actions, and relationships. A relationship with a taker is something that none of us strive to be involved in, yet it can happen as we seek out the give and take of friendship or intimacy.

A give and take relationship is not perfect, but it is based off of the reciprocity of investing emotional capital to the extent of balancing the effort between those involved. You invest some emotional capital and the other individual invests some emotional capital, so each person has a stake in the healthy relationship. This encourages balance and maintenance within the relationship, so that it will grow. These healthy relationships are wonderful, supportive, and important to have in your life, so that you are able to grow and help others grow. These are individuals that we choose to share our lives with, that we choose to be emotionally intimate with, out of an unspoken give and take agreement that exists innately within the relationship. Don't mistake this for a take only relationship that exists within the physical affections, it is an emotional vulnerability built off of trust.

The give and take relationship is important to have, but it is also prone to emotional hijack, where our perspectives and expectations are still flawed. We give our best efforts, but we are still limited in our knowledge and understanding of the inner workings of our give and take reciprocates. Feelings can still be hurt, misunderstandings can still be had, and living peaceably is still not a given - you are still striving to keep things balanced. The give and take relationship is healthy and wonderful, but still requires intentional attention to keep it that way. If both partners within this relationship keep the emotional capital investment at an equitable contribution, then you will experience a wonderfully intimate friendship, but there is one other type of relationship that transcends this give and take. The next level of healthy relationships is that of giving with no expectation of return.

Have you ever known the give only type of relationship? This is a relationship where one person, who is the unconditional giver, lays down their desires for the other person in the relationship. Think about it. The perspective is that this person, the giver, loves another so very much that they are willing to do anything, they are willing to put the other's needs before their own, without expectation of reciprocation. The giver's thoughts rest solely on the other person's wellbeing, even though that person may not see the whole picture, the giver already knows what the end should be and how to bring about a peaceable result. The feelings that follow these thoughts are of a pure love that flows out through their actions, demonstrating unconditional importance and value to the investment of their emotional capital. Their actions then become a type of conduct that undeniably confirms their thoughts and feelings and they gain a reputation for being the one that will go to no limit to pour all of their emotional capital into the relationship.

Think about giving with no expectation of return and what kind of relationship would result as a result of this intention. Imagine if both individuals in the relationship were to attempt to live this way and invest their emotional capital in this manner – the results would be exponential! If two people give to one another without expectation of return, something amazing happens! The relationship reaches new levels of importance and value, where trust, strength, and forgiveness lay at the core. This type of relationship is not something that we can just manifest out of thin air, but it is an intentional direction of our efforts to pour out our emotional capital, which makes us extremely vulnerable, but then, so is the other person. The expectation of receiving nothing in return develops something curious within our perspective, something that transforms our perspective into a patient acceptance of the other individual. It is at this point that nothing surprises us or falls short of our expectations, therefore the emotional hijack throttles way down and takes a back seat. This is when we can choose our thoughts, our feelings, and actions, thereby choosing how we will conduct ourselves, and choosing our reputation. How wonderful would this choice be?! So how can we as a flawed people get to this level?

If you were training for a major competition, who would you seek to learn from? Would you grab just anyone off the street? Of course not! If you were a collegiate athlete you would not pick your next door neighbor, who just might happen to be a junior high coach. Even if your next door neighbor is the nicest person alive, they still don't coach to the level that you would need in order to be competitive at the collegiate level. If you are going to win the top prize, then you need to learn from the very best, right? That way it will be worth it when you go through all of the time, effort, sacrifice, and pain, while you subject your body to all of the demands that this training puts on it. You would contract the best coach that you could find, then train diligently under their guidance. This coach knows the secrets of your opponents, they know the tactics that your opponents will use to throw you off balance, and they know how to make you the best that you can be, so that you will win the competition. There are high stakes here!

Some of the highest stakes are in the realm of emotional capital investment, where you are not just working to obtain a prize of healthy relationships, you are striving for the prize of living a peaceable life! If anything is like a competition, it is the struggle of maintaining healthy relationships and living this life peaceably! Sometimes it seems like a never ending endurance race, where you are putting one foot in front of the other, testing your mental fortitude, because you cannot yet see where the finish line rests. Other times it is a chess match, full of strategy and anticipation, where one wrong move can lead to the end of the competition. Sometimes it is an all-out sprint, causing you to push with everything you have towards the prize that is set before you. Through all of our struggles, there is One that we can look to as the example, the mentor, the counselor, the one who did it perfectly.

There was someone that made a mark on history with such an impact, that all time is now measured by His life. This is a person that laid down His life, gave sacrificially, and did not expect anything in return – in fact, He expected that some would reject what He had done for them. He loved with such intensity and fervor, but was gentle and meek. His life demonstrated importance and value to the entire world and His death demonstrated His unconditional love to each and every one of us. There is one that was willing and able to live a perfect life through his every thoughts, feeling, and action, something that no one else could ever do, where we are all flawed and not perfect, all of us missing the mark of perfection. He is the gold standard of how to give without expecting anything in return. He is our perfect template for the demonstration of importance and value.

If we are to live in such a manner that our flawed perspective does not lead towards flawed expectations, thoughts, feelings, actions, conduct, and reputation, then we must align our perspective with the perfect template of demonstrating importance and value. We must realize that we cannot do this on our own and seek Him for His guidance, in order to live in this manner each and every day, throughout all of our interactions. We must seek Him so that we may demonstrate our core values through our actions and ward off the potential for the emotional hijack. How wonderful a life would we lead if we sought to give unconditionally, with no expectation of return?! Where would we be now if we had lived this way all along? What impact would this have on all of our relationships? There is only one issue: we have all missed the mark of perfection, we are all flawed, and we have limited emotional capital.

So with limits on our emotional capital, how on earth can we live this way day in and day out? The difficulty is who to select to give unconditionally and exponentially multiply our emotional capital, because another flawed person would only get us so far, we need someone with unlimited access. To give unconditionally to all that we meet will result in a drainage that we cannot refill on our own, but if we are in a relationship with another giver, then there is a way to access unlimited and exponential emotional capital! We must seek out our perfect template! The One who did it all perfectly is the One whom we need to seek out and learn from. Jesus Christ is the One who laid His life down on the cross for you and for me. No matter what you believe, it is undeniable that Jesus' actions demonstrated true importance and value to everyone around Him; even to the entire world. Those that follow Him know that once we call Him Lord and seek His forgiveness for our sin, then He is faithful and just to forgive us and can make us whole again. Through that redemption He demonstrates that we are important and valuable to Him. Even the other religious leaders through time have acknowledged Jesus' impact on the world. This is the One that can give unlimited emotional capital and will multiply your emotional capital beyond limit, so seek Him out!

This was my most vital finding of all, that until we give our lives over to Jesus Christ, we will always have a flawed perspective. Until we bring our perspectives into alignment through Christ, we will always view the world through the lens of a flawed individual. This lens cannot be corrected by our own efforts, but it will remain flawed, until we view the world through the lens of the One who sees without flaw. In archery, when you miss the bullseye, aka the perfect shot, it is called sin – our flaws cause us to miss the mark of perfection, resulting in sin. If we are going to set things right, then we need to start with admitting that we are a flawed people that miss the mark (or sin), and we cannot hit the mark of perfection on our own. We cannot do anything to save ourselves from our sin and our flaws will cause us to spend eternity out of His presence, the One who is perfect, being fully just and fully

God. We need to acknowledge that Jesus Christ completed the work that we could not, that He did it perfectly and we accept His sacrifice to pay for our sins. We must ask Him to come into our hearts and be the Lord of our life, be the One that guides us and leads us in ways that we do not understand. Jesus Christ competed at a level that none of us can attain to and He freely offers to make us whole again, so that we may compete at a level like no other. He freely offers us the way to align our perspectives to produce a new life full of right thinking, right feeling, right actions, right conduct, and a right reputation.

If you have completed every interaction perfectly up to this point, then I would strongly suggest that you have not had any interactions at all, but have been living under a rock with little to no friends. We are all flawed, so if we are to live a life that is not prone to constant emotional hijack and relationship repair, then we need the resource with unlimited emotional capital. If you are tired of coming up short of emotional capital, then I would highly recommend that you surrender your life over to Jesus Christ, the One who can make you whole again. If you want to continue to live a flawed life, repeating the same mistakes over and over, then that is completely up to you. However, if you consider each of your interactions from the previous Chapters, you must admit that there would be a significant impact upon each if you gave unconditionally without expectation of return.

I had lived my life for myself for a very long time, knowing all along that Jesus Christ was the answer to all of my questions, but I was willingly blind to it. I was in denial because I only had an occasional give and take relationship, but at the core I was a stone cold taker. Due to my flawed perspectives I never became truly emotionally intimate with anyone, resulting in a mess that was now my life. This produced very unhealthy relationships with everyone, even with my family who loved me. I remember that I was in my sophomore year of college when I had experienced yet another break up, fully drained of all of my emotional capital and ready to just be done with this life. I couldn't sleep, so as the thoughts of despair crept into feelings of hopelessness, I decided to get up and go for a drive at 2:00am in the morning.

As I got into my Nissan pickup, I paused, almost going back into bed to toss and turn some more, but the hopelessness nudged me to start the truck and drive. As I pulled onto route 1, I decided to go to the one place that would make me feel a little better, despite all of the carnage that I had caused. I drove the dark and winding roads to a small beach that I frequented quite often - it was a public beach that was only on the local radar. I was confident that I would be alone on the sand. I smiled as I got closer, because I could see the parking lot was empty and I knew that I was the only one there. I parked my truck and got out to inhale a deep breath of the ocean air. Normally I would just relax at this moment, but I was still in torment over how this mess was apparently the new normal for all of my relationships.

The more that I mulled over the chaos that I had caused, the greater the level of hopelessness grew, opening a door for despair creep in. This continued until an irrational thought slipped subtly into my mind – what about swimming out into the open ocean as far as you can go and just giving up. I thought about it for a moment. What if I did? My truck would be found the next day and all anyone would know is that I ditched them and just left. Their lives would probably be better anyways, without me to screw it up. After all, my body wouldn't wash up on the beach until quite sometime later. Even then, the fish would have most likely taken care of the identifying marks – I'll just have to make sure that I swim out extra far. I started towards the water and I paused for a moment.

To this day, it still strikes me odd that I paused, because once I made up my mind, I usually followed through, but something stopped me. Someone stopped me. The thoughts of giving up became thoughts of giving over control, after all, I wasn't doing so hot, but who would I give it over to? Who would even want to deal with it all? All of a sudden I became angry at everything that I had done and extremely frustrated with myself and my choices. I wasn't ready to give up anymore! I was ready to fight, but what or who? I was an emotional hijack personified! Round and round went my emotions and my thoughts spun and reeled, until finally I looked up at the sky and yelled out loud. No idea why. But I yelled with everything that was within me and started to pace back and forth on the beach. It was a good thing that no one was there, because they would have called the police for disturbing the peace!

I then stopped, looked up again, and it hit me! I knew who said He would always be there and never forsake me! I cried out, "Okay God. If you're there, then I give up! You win! I gave my life over to you back when I was a kid, but I know that I didn't give it all over to you and now it's a mess! So you can have it! I'm done with it all! I'm done with women! I'm done with trying to figure this out! I'm just done! Just take it! I tell you what! I will give you a year to see if you can do better than I have! I give up!" I sat down in a sweaty heap, actually feeling relieved. It was odd, but peaceful… oddly peaceful. So after a while, I quietly got up, went back to my truck, and drove back home to crawl into my bed at 3:30am, only to sleep solidly for the first time in a long time. I got up the next morning feeling like a huge burden had been lifted – no more hopelessness, no more despair, just thoughts of wondering how God is going to work. I had feelings of peace, but my actions hadn't fully followed suit at that point. There were many trials to come and many hardships to face, but I found that as I began to read His Word, I was able to build a healthy relationship with Him. Seeking out Jesus and giving my life over to His reign resulted in a very full life, overflowing with healthy relationships based off of giving unconditionally without expectation.

This is my testimony of His work in my life. He accomplished things that I could not. He worked to correct my flawed lens with the lens of His Word to make my perspective more like His, my expectations more like His, my thoughts, feelings, actions, conduct, and reputation more like His. I could not do this on my own. I need the perfect template to guide me through each and every day, making me into a new creation. I am still flawed and I still get emotionally hijacked, but that's when I've put down His lens and I'm trying to make things happen in my own efforts. That's when I fail. As soon as I realize what I have done, I turn from my own flawed efforts and put on His lens. I share all of this with you so that you will know that I struggled on my own, creating a mess of my life, but you and I don't have to struggle on our own anymore. We have free access to the One perfect template. You too can have the fullness of life that Jesus brings to your relationship with Him, as He guides you and leads you.

Final Exercise:

1. Take your previous list of 4 interactions from Chapter 4's exercise.

2. Define the type of relationship that each represents from your side: taker only, give and take, give only.

3. Define the type of relationship that each represents from their side: taker only, give and take, give only.

4. Is this the type of relationship that you want to keep going? Why?

5. What do you need to do to keep the emotional capital growing in each of these relationships? Is it worth it?

6. Have you ever considered that you can't do this all on your own and need help beyond your circle of family and friends? Have you sought counseling? From whom?

7. Have you ever had a coach that was excellent? What were some of the things that they did that set them apart to be particularly effective in your training?

8. Do you have a personal relationship with someone that gives unconditionally? What is that like? What do you like about it? Do you desire to spend more time with them? What can you do to become more like that person?

9. If you are tired of the unhealthy relationships in your life, then you need the help of someone who is not flawed. You know who I am talking about. If you are ready to surrender your life and let God take over, then continue reading.

The following scriptures are from the New King James Version of the Bible and they outline the plan of salvation through faith in Jesus Christ.

Romans 3:23 – for all have sinned and fall short of the glory of God.

Romans 3:10 – As it is written: "There is none righteous, no, not one;

Romans 5:12 – Therefore, just as through one man sin entered the world, and death through sin, and thus death spread to all men, because all sinned–

Romans 6:23– For the wages of sin [is] death, but the gift of God [is] eternal life in Christ Jesus our Lord.

Romans 5:8– But God demonstrates His own love toward us, in that while we were still sinners, Christ died for us.

Romans 10:9-10 – that if you confess with your mouth the Lord Jesus and believe in your heart that God has raised Him from the dead, you will be saved. For with the heart one believes unto righteousness, and with the mouth confession is made unto salvation

Romans 10:13 – For "whoever calls on the name of the LORD shall be saved."

Romans 10:17 – So then faith [comes] by hearing, and hearing by the word of God.

These scriptures point out that we have all missed the mark of perfection, that we have all fallen short and cannot conquer death on our own. The death that we must all acknowledge is that of an eternal separation from the God of all creation, but by Jesus Christ's death on the cross, He has made the only way for us to have access to eternal life. He has died of His own free will and offered this free gift of salvation to all who surrender their lives over to His Lordship by confessing with their mouth and believing in their heart that Jesus Christ is the Lord of their lives and that God the Father has raised Him from the dead. If you believe this in your heart, then call upon His name for salvation, by repeating the following out loud:

"Lord Jesus, I am a sinner and I cannot save myself. I believe that you are the Son of God, who died on the cross for my sins, was buried, and rose again on the third day. By faith, I receive your free gift of salvation to eternal life. I want you to be the Lord of my life and that you would come into my heart and make me a new creation as my Lord and Savior. Amen"

If you have said this prayer, congratulations! I applaud your willingness to take this most vital step of all in surrendering your life to the Perfect Template. I encourage you to find a Bible believing church that is local and can help you grow in your knowledge and faith in the Lord Jesus Christ!

Again, this is my most vital finding of all. Until we give our lives over to Jesus Christ, we will always have a flawed perspective, because we will always view the world through the lens of a flawed individual. It is not easy to strive to live peaceably, but through the redeeming work of Jesus Christ, we are able to form healthy relationships, based off of giving unconditionally, without expectation of return. We don't have to be stuck in the mess of our lives, once we surrender them to the perfect template, Jesus Christ. I had hoped to answer the question that Jay had proposed, but it seems as though I have only just scratched the surface. By further study of the perfect template, Jesus Christ, I would learn so much more than I could ever imagine! He has brought a fullness of life that I had not thought possible! I pray that you will find the same fullness of life that I have through His redeeming work in your life!

www.ingramcontent.com/pod-product-compliance
Lightning Source LLC
Chambersburg PA
CBHW070824260726
48660CB00005B/1981